# A PROVEN, ACTIVE, FAITHFUL WALK

## A STUDY ON THE BOOK OF JAMES

STACY DAVIS & BRENDA HARRIS

## EDITORIAL TEAM

**PASTOR CHRIS SWANSEN**
Theological Editor,
Calvary Chapel Chester Springs

**PASTOR STEVEN DORR**
Pastoral Support,
Calvary Chapel Chester Springs

**CARINNA LAROCCO**
Copy Editor

**JOAN PURDY**
Copy and Content Editor

**MELISSA BEREDA**
Graphic Designer

**ANGELA ANDES**
**MARIE GAY**
**DIANE MORROW**
**ALLYSON ROSENBERGER**
**SUE ROSSITER**
Focus Group

**LYNN JENSEN**
Office Support

**CHRIS GOOD**
Photographer/Media Support

**DANIELLE ROSSNEY**
Video Support

**A PROVEN, ACTIVE, FAITHFUL WALK**
A Study on the Book of James
Part of the Delighting in the Lord Bible Study Series

© Copyright 2021
Calvary Chapel Chester Springs
PO Box 595, Eagle, PA 19480

ISBN 979 853 702 7645

Cover Design: Melissa Bereda
Cover Photo: IStock Getty Images: baon

Printed in the United States of America

## TABLE OF CONTENTS

*Stacy Davis*

Stacy has been teaching women God's Word for over 15 years. She has learned many Biblical truths through difficult trials. Beginning at the age of three with her mother's brain aneurism, to the death of her fourth son and through invasive breast cancer, Stacy's faith has been tried and tested many times over. Her life gives testimony to God's redeeming and transforming power. Stacy teaches the truths of God's Word with passion, desiring to share with all women how to go through everyday struggles victoriously in Jesus Christ. She lives in PA with her husband, Barclay. They have six children.

*Brenda Harris*

Brenda's background in education, along with her many years as a classroom teacher, was foundational for the plans God had for her to serve Him. In 2006, she transitioned away from instructing young people how to read literature and began teaching women how they can have a closer walk with the Lord through reading and studying their Bible. She is an enthusiastic teacher who loves a great visual to help demonstrate practical ways to apply God's Word to real life. Brenda lives in PA with her husband, Michael, and their two children.

But he who looks into the perfect law of liberty and continues in it, and is not a forgetful hearer but a doer of the work, this one will be blessed in what he does.

James 1:25

5

## OUR APPROACH TO GOD'S WORD

To get the most out of this study, you will want to ensure the time you are studying God's Word is not just an academic exercise, but is for your personal application and life transformation. The goal of studying God's Word is to know God; who He is, what He has done, and why this is important for you. Studying the Bible should increase your faith in God. As you read the Bible, God is interacting with you. Your study time becomes a life-giving, life-changing experience, not just head knowledge. However, God's Word can only be personal and life-changing when the Spirit of the Living God is in your heart (John 14:17).

As soon as this spiritual transformation takes place in your heart, the Holy Spirit communicates with your spirit all the Truths found in God and made known through Jesus Christ.

Jesus is the only way to be born of the spirit and have eternal life. This is how the study of God's Word becomes personal. It begins with a personal relationship through faith in Jesus Christ. If you've never accepted Jesus as your Lord and Savior, turn to the Delighting in My Salvation page of this study. This is your first step.

## THE R.E.A.D. APPROACH

All of the Delighting in the Lord studies use a study model we developed called R.E.A.D. This model takes you from reading the verses, to experiencing and understanding the details of the verses, on to applying them to your life, and finishing with delighting in God. The DITL studies are all verse-by-verse in their approach, allowing Scripture to interpret Scripture as you study. Our hope in writing these studies is that you will learn to understand the Bible and the heart of God.

Each week of study takes you through the R.E.A.D. approach. The week begins with an introduction that includes a real person whose life exemplifies the verses in the lesson.

### Prayer

Luke 24:45 tells us that "He [Jesus] opened their understanding, that they might comprehend the Scriptures." After Jesus rose from the dead, He appeared before His disciples on numerous occasions. He spoke these words to them shortly before ascending into heaven. Jesus helped them understand the Scriptures; all that had been written in the Law of Moses, the Prophets, and the Psalms to that point.

It is the same for us. Jesus will open our understanding to the Bible.

For this reason, we encourage you to start in prayer every time you approach God's Word. Ask God to open your mind to His understanding, to make His Word clear to you, and to reveal to you an understanding of who He is.

## RECEIVING GOD'S WORD

With each week of study, start by reading the designated verses from beginning to end. This will help you understand the big picture of what is being said as well as see the context. You may see consistencies, repeated words, and themes being developed. Read slowly and thoughtfully.

## EXPERIENCING GOD'S WORD

The Experiencing portion is where you will interact with God through His Word to gain spiritual understanding. This section will help you answer the questions, "Who, what, where, when, and why." To do this you will go verse-by-verse answering inductive and deductive questions. You will observe details, see connections, and interpret what is being said within context so that you can draw conclusions. There might also be questions that have you looking in other books of the Bible. Our hope is for you to see God's cohesive voice throughout Scripture.

Each week's verses are usually broken into smaller sections called Experience 1, Experience 2, and so forth. You may choose to do all of these sections at one sitting or space them out throughout the week.

## ACTING ON GOD'S WORD

In this part of the study, you will be applying the verses to your life. Hebrews 4:12 says, "For the word of God is living and powerful, and sharper than any two-edged sword, piercing even to the division of soul and spirit, and of joints and marrow, and is a discerner of the thoughts and intents of the heart." Through the Holy Spirit, God's Word will speak to the deep places of your life.

For this study, we've divided this section into three headings: Head, Heart, and Habit. In each of these areas you will examine personal applications relating to the themes and points in the Experiencing section of the study. Don't neglect this section. Be prayerful and allow God to speak to you personally.

## DELIGHTING IN GOD'S WORD

Our ministry's foundational verse is Psalm 27:4. This verse tells us to delight in the Lord's perfections and to meditate in His temple. In this final section, you will end by praising God for who He is.

### COMMITMENT AND PLANNING

Dedication and a time commitment will be needed to get the full benefit of this study. Plan on setting aside 1–2 hours a week to complete the whole week's study. You will find that your investment in God's Word will be seen in your spiritual growth. Plan on coming to study with your weekly lesson completed.

### BIBLE TRANSLATIONS

The DITL studies use the New King James version (NKJV) of the Bible when writing the study questions. You may find it easier to use this same translation. We recommend using a literal Bible translation such as KJV, NASB or ESV for the study if you don't use the NKJV.

### BIBLE COMMENTARIES AND RESOURCES

We recommend that you don't use any Bible commentaries or resources until after you have studied the weekly verses yourself, allowing the Holy Spirit to direct your understanding. It can be tempting to read the commentary in study Bibles and online. Give yourself time to understand what is being said in each verse before turning to resources. We promise you that God will give you light bulb moments in your study time as you dig into the verses yourself. If you find yourself struggling with a question, leave the answer blank and bring that question to your small group discussion time.

In the study you may notice references to Strong's Concordance. It may look something like this: *Firstborn* is *protokos* (Strong's G4416). When you see this, it means that we are giving you the original word used in either the Hebrew (Old Testament) or Greek (New Testament) so that you can better understand the word usage. This often helps give a deeper understanding of what is being said through the use of that word.

*Here are some suggested resources to use after you've completed each week's questions:*

- *The Bible Knowledge Commentary* by Walvoord and Zook
- Warren Wiersbe Commentaries
- www.blueletterbible.org
- *The New Strong's Exhaustive Concordance of the Bible*
- *Vine's Complete Expository Dictionary of Old and New Testament Words*

## Individual or Small Group:

The DITL studies can be used individually or with a group. If using on your own, we suggest doing the study pages over the course of a week then following up with the teaching video. If you are doing the study with a group, we recommend all ladies complete the study on their own throughout the week. When the ladies meet, break a large group into smaller ones; each group with a leader to guide the discussion. Following the small group time, watch the teaching video as one group or have the ladies watch later on their own.

## Teaching Videos:

A teaching video accompanies each week of the study. The video should be considered a capstone on your personal study time. It is meant to tie everything together and to give you some additional insights into the verses that were studied that week. The teaching videos are helpful but not required. The study is written to guide you deep into the verses yourself. Our goal is for you to gain understanding through the Holy Spirit and begin to learn on your own. Should you desire the teaching component of the study, our videos can be viewed on the ministry website: www.delightinginthelord.com. A free teaching video set can also be requested for groups by emailing info@delightinginthelord.com.

## Week 1 Format:

The first week of study is an introductory week. There is no homework, and the introductory video may be watched at the start of the study. There are Teaching Note pages for all the video lessons. For week one, these two pages are found at the beginning of the study. For all other weeks, they are found at the end of each week.

Let's get started!
We are so thrilled that you have chosen to study God's Word. There is truly nothing better you can be doing with your time. The benefit will overflow into all areas of your life as God works through you by the power of His Word. We are praying for you.

In Christ's love,
Stacy and Brenda

God desires a personal relationship with you. Maybe you've never heard that before. He loves you so much that He sent His Son, Jesus, to die on the cross for you. In His love for you, God provided His Son, Jesus Christ, to be the perfect sacrifice for your sin. When Jesus was crucified on the cross nearly 2,000 years ago, God put the sins of the whole world onto His perfect Son, Jesus, so that through Him you'd have forgiveness and eternal life. Jesus paid the penalty for your sin and provided a way to God.

The first step in receiving the forgiveness Jesus offers is by acknowledging you have lived your life apart from Him. You have followed your own motives and desires. In God's eyes, this is sin. Sin carries eternal consequences and separation from God. Salvation begins with repentance. Everyone must recognize they are sinful human beings in need of a Savior. Jesus is the answer to our sin problem. If you have never prayed to Jesus to ask Him into your heart, it is a simple prayer of acknowledging your faith in Jesus and asking Him to forgive you of your sins.

### THE CONVERSATION WITH GOD IS LIKE THIS...

*"Dear God, I admit I am a sinner and have lived my life doing what I want. You are perfectly holy, and I am not. My sin grieves You and separates me from You. Please forgive me."*

"For all have sinned and fall short of the glory of God." (Romans 3:23)

*"I believe that You provided Jesus Christ as the answer for my sin through His death on the cross. He paid my sin debt in full. He is my perfect substitute. Because of Him, I am cleansed forever from my sin."*

"For the wages of sin is death, but the gift of God is eternal life in Christ Jesus our Lord." (Romans 6:23)

*"Lord, please come into my heart and life. From this day forward, I desire to know You more and want to begin a personal relationship with You as my Savior and Lord. Thank You for Your free gift of salvation and that I am no longer separated from You but am filled with You by the power of the Holy Spirit."*

"If you confess with your mouth the Lord Jesus and believe in your heart that God has raised Him from the dead, you will be saved." (Romans 10:9)

*"Thank You, God, for forgiving me. Please help me to grow to know You better and to live a life that pleases You from this day forward. Amen."*

*If you have prayed to accept Christ as your Savior, please tell someone today! Share this exciting news with a close Christian friend, your small group leader, or your pastor. They will be thrilled to encourage you in your faith and your decision to follow Jesus!*

# WEEK 1
# INTRODUCTION TO JAMES

Teaching Title _____

_____

_____

_____

_____

_____

_____

_____

_____

_____

_____

_____

_____

_____

_____

_____

_____

_____

_____

_____

_____

_____

_____

Teaching Videos and handouts are available for free at www.delightinginthelord.com.

Teaching Title _____

_____

_____

_____

_____

_____

_____

_____

_____

_____

_____

_____

_____

_____

_____

_____

_____

_____

_____

_____

_____

_____

Teaching Videos and handouts are available for free at www.delightinginthelord.com.

**Before you begin this study, write down anything you already know about the book of James:**

## INTRODUCTION

James speaks simply, pointedly, and clearly to the Jewish believers at the time of his writing as well as anyone who has put their faith in Jesus Christ and takes the name "Christian." This small but mighty book is full of challenges, exhortations, and encouragements for every Christian. It is highly practical and leaves very few areas of our lives unexamined.

In five chapters James will challenge our faith and the way we live. His whole letter addresses the connection between inward faith in Jesus and the outward working of that faith. The two must go together. James states, "For as the body without the spirit is dead, so faith without works is dead also" (James 2:26). The gospel of Jesus Christ is woven into the letter without explicitly talking about the life, death, and resurrection of Jesus Christ. James will make the point clear that genuine saving faith found in Jesus Christ will produce good works.

James speaks with Pastoral tenderness to his readers, often calling them "beloved brethren," yet exhorts them to live a life that is faithful, pure, and submitted to God. He speaks of unity among believers and gives pointed words against favoritism and pride. He begins his letter by challenging our attitudes in trials and circles back to that topic as he ends his letter. He does this by speaking of the importance of prayer during times of suffering. He tells those who follow Christ to be a good example for others, to obey God, and to trust Him in all areas of life. You will be challenged to:

- Endure your trials with perseverance
- Avoid partiality
- Work toward unity; avoid division in the church
- Control what you say
- Trust God as the ultimate judge of unrighteousness

- Look at earthly wealth with eternity in mind
- Pursue Godly wisdom
- Pray over all things
- Care for those in need
- Have an eternal perspective

The book of James has been called a New Testament "how-to book" on the Christian life. Filled with practical, godly wisdom, like any good how-to book, James uses relatable illustrations for examples. He is more concerned with believers walking out their belief in Christ than a faith that shows no action. Because this is such an important part of the book of James, in the Acting section of each week's lesson, you will complete a "head, heart, and habits" reflection. This portion of the lesson will encourage you to examine what the scriptures taught. Then you will be asked to seek God for any inconsistencies in your life. Finally, you will be challenged to see how God will develop new habits in you so that your faith is evident in all areas of your life.

## AUTHOR

It is widely held that James, the oldest half-brother of Jesus, was the author (Mark 6:3). Interestingly, James doesn't point out this fact. He refers to himself as a "bondservant of God and the Lord Jesus Christ" (James 1:1). As Jesus' half-brother, he would have witnessed Jesus' earthly ministry as well as seen firsthand how Jesus handled family relationships. Jesus' perfect example, no doubt, made an impression on James, but it didn't immediately affect his faith.

Scripture tells us that James first rejected Jesus as the Messiah in John 7:5. It is likely that he did not put his faith in Jesus until after the resurrection. We are told in 1 Corinthians 15:7 that James was among those to see the risen Christ. Acts 1:14 says that he was among the disciples who met in the upper room for prayer following Jesus' ascension. It seems that glorious appearance made him believe, and James became a disciple of Christ. He was a part of the formation of the early church on Pentecost. He later became a prominent leader of the Jerusalem church and would preside over a debate in the church about circumcision (Acts 15:13). Paul recounted the Jerusalem Council in Galatians 2:1-10. He calls James a pillar in the church. Much of what Paul says is echoed in the book of James.

Known for his godliness and reverence to God, he has been nicknamed "James, the Just." He also bears the nickname "Old Camel Knees" for his devotion to God in prayer as evidenced in the book of James. Tradition holds that James was executed around 62 A.D.

## AUDIENCE

The letter begins by addressing "the twelve tribes scattered abroad." Different opinions exist about who these people were at the time. Since James is writing to believers about the connection between a person's faith and works, these twelve tribes are most likely Jewish-believing Christians. The word "brethren" is used 15 times when referring to his recipients. Additionally, James makes many allusions to the Old Testament. The scattered Jewish believers may have been dispersed after Stephen's stoning at the end of Acts 7, but more likely under Herod Agrippa I's persecution of Christians in Acts 12 around 44 A.D. This letter is also known as a "circular letter" which was typically passed from church to church. Despite its Jewish undertones, this letter is applicable for all believers.

## DATE WRITTEN

The book of James is believed to be possibly one of the earliest written books of the New Testament and was likely written between 45-50 A.D.

## MAP

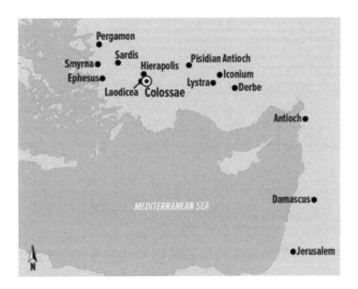

## AS YOU GET STARTED

*Summarize any information you gained after reading the introduction to James.*

*In the space below, write a prayer to the Lord about what you hope to gain from Him as you study the book of James.*

# WEEK 2
# A FAITH THAT OVERCOMES TRIALS

As dawn began to break, shards of light pierced into the darkness of Dmitri's dirty, cold prison cell. For seventeen years, every morning at daybreak he followed this exact routine; he rose from his bed, stood at attention, faced east, raised his hands in the air, and sang a praise song to Jesus in Russian. As Dmitri sang, jeers and scoffing came from the other fifteen hundred hardened criminals around him. They laughed, cursed, and threw things at him. However, this did not dissuade Dmitri from singing nor quench his strong, unwavering faith in Jesus Christ.

At a young age Dmitri's parents taught him about God and took him to church; however, as communism flourished in Russia, churches closed, and many pastors were either killed or imprisoned for practicing their faith. By the time Dmitri was an adult, the closest church was a three-day walk from his home. Because of this, Dmitri and his family began to worship God in their home. Before long, 150 people from his small village attended church services at Dimitri's home. When the local authorities became aware of Dmitri's "illegal church," persecution immediately came against him and his family. He lost his factory job and his wife lost her teaching job. Their sons were expelled from school. Dmitri would not stop meeting with others to worship God and eventually was taken to jail where he spent seventeen years of his life.

One day in prison the guards demanded Dmitri renounce his faith, or he would face execution. Dmitri would not turn his back on God. He was dragged from his cell to the center of the prison, and then suddenly the most incredible thing happened. "Before they [the guards and Dmitri] reached the door leading to the courtyard—before stepping out into the place of execution—fifteen hundred hardened criminals stood at attention by their beds. They faced the east, and they began to sing. Dmitri said that it sounded to him like the greatest choir in all of human history. Fifteen hundred criminals raised their arms and began to sing the 'Heart Song' that they had heard Dmitri sing to Jesus every morning for all of those years. Dimitri's jailers instantly released their hold on his arms and stepped away from him in terror. One of them demanded to know, 'Who are you?' Dmitri straightened his back and stood as tall and proud as he could. He responded: 'I am the son of the Living God, and Jesus is His name!' The guards returned him to his cell. Sometime later, Dmitri was released, and he returned to his family." (Nik Ripken, *The Insanity of God*, p. 158)

> GOD PROMISES TO GIVE WISDOM DURING A TRIAL. HE ASKS US TO TRUST HIM WITHOUT DOUBTING, KNOWING HE WILL ANSWER.

For most of us, Dmitri's trial is unfathomable. Here in the United States we do not typically face this kind of religious persecution. We might secretly wonder if we would be nearly as steadfast as Dmitri was if we ever faced such horrendous circumstances. Dmitri found joy in the midst of his dreadful trial because of his faith. When he focused on God instead of his unbearable circumstances, he was able to praise the One who was in control over his life. Unbeknown to him, his actions had been an example to the other prisoners who were watching and listening.

James chapter 1 begins by addressing the twelve tribes of Israel, who like Dmitri were separated from their home. James writes to encourage them to "count it all joy" when they fall into various trials as they wait patiently for God to move in their circumstances, knowing all trials have a purpose (James 1:4). God promises to give wisdom during a trial. He asks us to trust Him without doubting, knowing He will answer (James 1:5–6). Dmitri had times when he was tempted to give up, but as he endured, God solidified his faith to the point of even being willing to die for the sake of Christ. There is a reward for this kind of trust. James 1:12 describes this reward as a crown of life, which is enjoyed now and in the future. When Jesus is the foundation for our life and our faith is in Him, it is possible to find joy amidst hardship. God is the great stabilizer when everything around us is shifting and uncertain. We can trust Him and allow the difficulty to be an opportunity for growth. As you begin your study time, thank God for His provision of peace and His complete sovereignty over your everyday circumstances as well as your times of hardship. Ask Him to give you a faith that overcomes trials with joy.

## Receiving God's Word

**Open in Prayer**
Read James 1:1–18

## Experiencing God's Word

### EXPERIENCE 1: FAITH TESTED THROUGH TRIALS

James 1:1–11

1. Read James 1:1. James identifies himself as the author of this book. It is believed James is Jesus' half-brother born to Mary and Joseph. From Galatians 1:19, we know that Jesus had a half-brother named James. In James 1:1 he refers to himself as a "Bondservant of God and of the Lord Jesus Christ." In your own words explain how the word *bondservant* helps you understand James' relationship with God.

2. In James 1:1 we learn that James is writing to the "twelve tribes which are scattered." In Exodus 1:1–6 the twelve tribes are named. They are the children of the twelve sons of Jacob known as the Old Testament people of God. In Acts 2 the Jewish people were among the first who put their faith in Jesus Christ and formed the early church of believers. Read Acts 8:1–4. Why were they scattered?

a. Peter also wrote to this group of scattered Jewish believers. Read 1 Peter 1:1–2. How does Peter define these people? What do they all have in common?

## DEEPER EXPERIENCE

*"To the twelve tribes: What James meant by this reference to the twelve tribes is difficult to understand. The question is whether James wrote a letter to only Christians from a Jewish background or to all Christians. Certainly, this letter applies to all Christians; yet James probably wrote his letter before Gentiles were brought into the church, or at least before Gentile Christians appeared in any significant number." (Dave Guzik, Enduring Word commentary from blueletterbible.org)*

## DEEPER EXPERIENCE

*"James was the head Pastor of the Jerusalem church, according to Acts 15, so his congregation would be mostly Jewish." (Pastor Chris Swansen, Calvary Chapel Chester Springs)*

b. Before we go any further in the book of James, it is important to understand the basis for our faith. Just as the book of James was written to the believing Jews, it is also written for each one of us. This book is written to those who have put their faith in Jesus Christ. If you have never put your faith in Jesus, turn to Delighting in My Salvation on page 10 and learn what Christ has done for you.

3. Read James 1:2–4 and answer the following questions:

   a. As you read James 1:2, the word *trial* is used in some Bible translations whereas in others the word *temptation* is used. Both words are *peirasmos* in the Greek (Strong's G3986). These words are synonyms for one another and refer to a trial where God is the agent for the purpose of proving someone's faith is genuine. It is never for the purpose of causing that person to fall. In verse 2 we find a strange command given to believers who were suffering various trials. What is the command?

   b. The word *joy* is *chara* in the Greek (Strong's G5479). It means calm delight. When trials happen, how does faith built upon Christ make this expression of joy possible according to verse 3–4?

## JESUS' EXAMPLE

*Hebrews 12:1–2 tells us that Jesus went to the cross with joy. As He endured the most unimaginable physical pain and suffering, He did it with joy. Jesus knew His death would save all sinners who believed in Him. Jesus endured the cross, He despised the shame, rose from the dead, and then sat down at the right hand of the throne of God.*

   c. The word *patience* is the word *hupomone* in Greek (Strong's G5281). It means to have a steadfastness in your faith. It describes a person not moved by their circumstances because they know they have a deliberate purpose. From verses 3–4, how do patience and faith work together so we can overcome trials?

## JESUS' EXAMPLE

*Despite the constant rejection and criticism from the Jewish religious leadership, Jesus never strayed from His God-given purpose. He said in John 6:38, "For I have come down from heaven, not to do my own will, but the will of Him who sent Me." Jesus was steadfast in His trust in God because He knew it had an eternal purpose.*

4. Read the following verses and note what you learn about why God allows trials in our lives:

   John 9:1–5

   2 Corinthians 12:9–10

   Hebrews 12:5–11

   1 Peter 1:6–9

   1 Peter 4:12–16

5. Read James 1:5–8. During trials wisdom is needed. Answer the following questions based on these verses:

   a. Who should we go to for wisdom? (v. 5)

   b. How is wisdom given? (v.5)

   c. What should be the condition of our faith when seeking wisdom? (v. 6)

d. Explain what it means to be "double-minded" in verse 7–8. How is the double-minded man described?

e. How is being double-minded a hindrance to receiving wisdom? (v. 7)

6. Read James 1:9–11. Contrast the poor and the rich man as they face trials. How can both men glory in their difficult circumstances? Why?

## JESUS' EXAMPLE

*When Jesus taught, He often turned normal thinking about life and its circumstances upside down by challenging His disciples to approach things differently. In Matthew 5:1–12 He gave a heavenly perspective saying, "Blessed are the poor in spirit, for theirs is the kingdom of heaven." Regarding suffering and persecution, He said, "Blessed are those who are persecuted for righteousness' sake, for theirs is the kingdom of heaven. Blessed are you when they revile and persecute you, and say all kinds of evil against you falsely for My sake. Rejoice and be exceedingly glad, for great is your reward in heaven, for so they persecuted the prophets who were before you." Jesus knew that the blessed and fulfilled life was one that kept eternity in focus despite physical circumstances.*

## EXPERIENCE 2: OVERCOMING OUR TRIALS

James 1:12–18

1. Read James 1:12. James uses the word *temptation* in this verse. The Greek word for temptation is *peirasmos* (Strong's G3986). It is the same word that James used in James 1:2. Remember from question 3a of Experience 1 that this word can also be defined as a trial allowed by God to prove something. How is the person in verse 12 described? How does God reward this person?

   a. Read Titus 3:4–6. The crown of life can often be confused with salvation. What do the verses in Titus say about salvation? Is the crown of life salvation? Explain.

### *DEEPER EXPERIENCE*

*"Verse 12 has in view the tried and tested believer who is assured of blessing as he endures grief for Christ's sake. When the temptation is over and he has remained steadfast until the end, he is promised the crown of life, which the Lord will bestow upon all who have shown by the devotion to Him that they truly loved Him. This is not to be confounded with eternal life, which is the free gift of God, the portion of all who believe in the Lord Jesus Christ."* (H. A. Ironside, James and 1 and 2 Peter, p.16)

2. Read James 1:13. We've learned that God has a plan for the trials He allows in our lives. The word *tempted* is used in this verse. That word in the Greek is *peirazo* (Strong's G3985) which means to tempt, to test, to prove or to solicit evil. What truth do you learn about God in this verse?

3. According to James 1:14 how do personal desires influence our response in a trial?




4. Read 1 John 2:15–17. What three human lusts entice us to sin? How do these lusts affect the way we go through a trial?




## JESUS' EXAMPLE

*Shortly after Jesus' baptism, Matthew 4:1 tells us that Jesus was led to the wilderness by the Spirit to be tempted by the devil. Deprived of food for 40 days, in a physically weakened state, Jesus stood against temptation. The devil tempted Jesus by enticing Him through the three human lusts of what feels good, looks good, and feeds the human ego. Jesus didn't waiver. He didn't give into His humanity but fought the devil by using the Word of God and stood strong.*


5. Read James 1:15 then fill in the blanks below regarding the progression of sin.

   Desire is_____ → gives birth to _____ → sin becomes full

   grown→ brings _____. (NKJV)


   a. Death is referred to in verse 15 as a result of sin. Read Romans 6:20–23. Describe how Jesus is the answer to our sin and death problem.

6. Read James 1:16–17. James told believers not to be deceived about who God is and His purposes with trials. How is God described in these verses?

a. How can these truths benefit a believer during a trial?

7. Read James 1:18 and answer the following questions:

a. What is the greatest gift that God has given to all people?

b. How was this gift given?

c. For those who receive this gift, what is God's goal toward us?

8. Let's look at this idea of firstfruits as seen in James 1:18. To gain further understanding read 1 Corinthians 15:20–23. Describe how Jesus is the firstfruit.

a. From these verses, how is a believer's life a kind of firstfruit as well?

9. This idea of firstfruits began in the Old Testament regarding the Jewish people. In Exodus 23:16 & 19 the Israelites were instructed by God to give the firstfruits of their harvest to Him as an offering. This was known as the Feast of the Harvest. The firstfruits were considered the best. This offering not only acknowledged that all they had belonged to God but also was an act of thanksgiving. It also anticipated the coming harvest from that crop. Using what James said about trials, God's gifts, and firstfruits, how does our life represent a firstfruit to the Lord as we exercise faith in trials?

10. Summarize what you learned about a faith that overcomes trials.

## ACTING ON GOD'S WORD

Trials in life are never easy. They are often uncomfortable, challenging, and can wear us down. We learned in James 1:1–18 that God uses them in the life of the believer to test our faith in Jesus Christ while achieving His purposes in our lives. Our faith in Jesus should fuel our focus in trying times as well as our response. We learned that God wants you to be complete in Him, lacking nothing to endure times of hardship and suffering. And yet, temptation is always trying to entice us to sin against God and blame Him. It isn't God who tempts us; it comes through our sinful nature. God has blessings He desires to give us as we go through times of testing with faith in Him.

We are all familiar with hardships. Maybe you just came out of a time of testing or maybe you are currently in one. One thing we know for sure; whether past or present, trials will keep coming. Did you learn something from James 1:1–18 that you can apply to a current situation or maybe something that will help you with whatever difficulty may come in the future?

Our study on James will break the "Acting" section into three parts each week. It will focus on the head, the heart, and the godly habits that God wants to develop in each believer as we walk out our faith in Him. The Head section will look at what you learned. The Heart section will ask questions about what God may be speaking to your heart about your attitudes. The Habit section asks specific questions about putting our faith in action. We encourage you to spend some time here as our tendency may be to skip over this section because it is personal and requires something of us. However, this is where we get to apply what we've learned so please don't miss this important step in the study.

## HEAD | What do I know?

1. Is there anything you learned about God from James 1:1–18?

2. Is there anything you learned about overcoming trials that you can apply to your most recent struggle in life?

## HEART | How is God moving in my heart?

1. How did God encourage you from James 1:1–18?

2. Can you identify any sin that God is exposing in your life as you studied these verses? What is He asking you to do? Explain.

3. How have you been prompted to pray? Write your prayer to the Lord below.

**HABIT**   How is God asking me to live out my faith?

1. How are you going to approach trials differently based on what you learned today? List specific ways you would like to change.

2. What is one thing you can do this week to apply what you learned from this lesson?

## DELIGHTING IN GOD'S WORD

As you end this week's lesson, write down a verse that God has impressed upon your heart throughout the week and pray it back to the Lord.

Teaching Title _____

_____

_____

_____

_____

_____

_____

_____

_____

_____

_____

_____

_____

_____

_____

_____

_____

_____

_____

_____

_____

Teaching Videos and handouts are available for free at www.delightinginthelord.com.

Teaching Title _____

_____

_____

_____

_____

_____

_____

_____

_____

_____

_____

_____

_____

_____

_____

_____

_____

_____

_____

_____

_____

_____

Teaching Videos and handouts are available for free at www.delightinginthelord.com.

# WEEK 3
# A FAITH THAT HEARS AND OBEYS THE WORD

The place was now a little too familiar. After the first time here, Mark never wanted to return. The night had been a blur, and he couldn't remember how exactly he found himself in this place again. His mind stumbled through the memories as he tried to piece it all together; the years of loneliness, his failing marriage, the drinking, and a numbness that got him through each day.

His marriage had been difficult from the beginning. Alcohol was his companion; his first love. His wife knew it, but Mark had become really good at hiding his addiction. Numbed each day by drunkenness, he managed to get by as a functioning alcoholic. The workday rolled into happy hour each night and then repeated the next day. When his wife found a credit card bill totaling over ten thousand dollars in bar-related charges, she demanded he change. But Mark wasn't interested in changing. Alcohol was his friend. He didn't want his wife telling him what he could and couldn't do. So, Mark picked his first love, alcohol, and left his wife and their two small children. Shortly after, a divorce ensued. Mark's life quickly spiraled downhill as his drinking increased. There were many nights of heavy drinking which led to blacking out and too many mornings of finding himself in random places with only sketchy memories of the night before.

On this particular morning Mark found himself in a cold, barren holding tank at the local jail. Surrounded by 40 or so other criminals, he felt the room was closing in on him. His mind was fuzzy. He grasped for details from the night before, and they slowly came back in pieces; the median, the oncoming traffic, the police lights, the sobriety test, and the metal handcuffs slapped on his wrists with another DUI issued in his name. But this morning was different from all the rest; something gnawed deep within him as Mark began to recognize the life he was living was a sham. No amount of alcohol would cover up that truth.

> GOD'S WORD EMPOWERS US TO LIVE OUT OUR FAITH AND TO OBEY GOD.

There were a bunch of empty cells adjoining the main holding tank where Mark sat. He wanted to be alone. He walked into one of the cells to get away from everyone. The room was brightly lit and held nothing more than a long metal bench that ran alongside the wall. Mark sat down trying to collect his thoughts. Interestingly, his thoughts turned toward God as his heart cried out, "What am I doing with my life, God?"

From his childhood, Mark knew about God. Growing up as a Catholic, his father had been very private about his faith; yet, Mark had vivid memories of his dad reading his Bible each day in the early morning hours. He watched his dad serve the community, but never wanted his charitable giving to be seen by others; it was between him and God. When Mark was a young teenager, his dad had him memorize Matthew 22:36–39, "'Teacher, which is the great commandment in the Law?' Jesus said to him, 'You shall love the Lord your God with all your heart and with all your soul and with all your mind. This is the first and great commandment. And the second is like it: You shall love your neighbor as yourself.'"

On his sixteenth birthday, Mark's dad gave him a Bible. Inside the cover was written, "I hope the Bible becomes part of your life. The truth in the Bible will help you in this life, more importantly this will show you how to have eternal life with our Creator. I want to share eternal life with you."

As Mark sat in that jail cell, God met him in a personal way. The foundation of Truth given to him all those years ago became real. The Word of God became real as he surrendered his life to Christ. Mark heard the Lord say to him, "Mark, you are going to walk out of this jail cell and never drink again." He did just that. When Mark was released from jail, he joined a Bible-focused addiction recovery program at his local non-denominational church and began not only reading his Bible but living it. As his love for God and the Word continues to grow, it becomes easier to make the choice each day to obey all of God's commands and live his life for the Lord. Today, after ten years, Mark has been sober and committed to never drinking alcohol again.

In James 1:19–27 James continues to give his counsel to believers who are facing trials of all kinds. He emphasizes the importance of God's Word in their lives during difficulties. When our love for God and His Word is implanted in our heart and received with meekness, we are able to walk through trials unspotted by the world and its temptations. God's Word empowers us to live out our faith and to obey God. Mark is my (Stacy's) brother-in-law, and I share his story with his permission. His life exemplifies a life changed by the Word of God; a life that did not just hear the Word growing up but also chose to receive it in the midst of his greatest struggle. He is now a doer of the Word by not returning to a life of alcoholism. His greatest joy is to help others going through the same struggle and pointing them to the saving power of Jesus Christ.

May we, too, not only hear the Word of God but choose to obey it in all areas of life. As we study the Word, may we look deep into the heart of God and not only see Jesus but be changed from the inside out and live a life that glorifies Him.

## Receiving God's Word

**Open in Prayer**
Read James 1:19–27

## Experiencing God's Word

### EXPERIENCE 1: POWER OF THE WORD IN TRIALS

1. James 1:19 begins with the word "so" showing its connection with verses 1–18. There is a theme that James developed in the preceding verses which ties into verses 19–27. Let's review before we begin.

   a. Reread James 1:18. God chose to give people both eternal and abundant life through Jesus Christ. How did God do this?

   b. To reinforce this point, read Romans 10:17 and write it below.

   c. Look over James 1:18–23. What word do you see repeated? Write it below. Why is this word important to note regarding our salvation and our sanctification?

### DEEPER EXPERIENCE

*"Ultimately the key both to responding to trials and resisting temptation is to be found in one's reaction to God's Word. Receptivity to the Word, responsiveness to the Word, and resignation to the Word are essential to spiritual growth. One must accept God's Word, act on it, and abide by it."* (Bible Knowledge Commentary, p. 822)

2. Read James 1:19 and then fill in the blanks below. Keep in mind this command is being given to those who are in trials as studied in James 1:1–18.

   Be_____ to hear, _____ to speak, _____ to wrath. (NKJV)

a. We often look at this verse only in regard to how we interact with others. However, knowing that these verses focus on trials, how does this verse address our interactions with God and His Word when in a trial?

3. Read James 1:20. The wrath of man is described as anger, violent passion, vengeance, and indignation (Strong's G3709). When the commands of verse 19 are not followed, what results according to verse 20?

a. Anger, violent passion, vengeance, and indignation can arise easily in the midst of a difficulty. James wants his readers to understand these are sins against God. How does the wrath of man hinder a believer in a trial?

4. James 1:19 contextually refers to our relationship with God but can carry over to our relationships with others. Read the following verses about listening to others, speaking cautiously, and staying calm. What do you learn?

Proverbs 10:19

Proverbs 14:17

Proverbs 16:32

Proverbs 17:27

## JESUS' EXAMPLE

*In John 8:1–11 an adulterous woman was brought before Jesus by the religious leadership. They came to Jesus to test Him and see if they could find a way to accuse Him of wrongdoing regarding the sin of this woman. As the leaders pressed in, wanting Jesus to condemn the woman for her sin, Jesus silently wrote something on the ground. Finally speaking, He said, "He who is without sin among you, let him throw a stone at her first." One by one, those who were accusing the woman walked silently away. In this example Jesus demonstrated how to be quick to listen, slow to speak, and slow to wrath.*

5.  Read James 1:21. James begins this verse with the word "therefore" as He makes some final points about how believers should walk through trials. He encourages his readers to lay aside ungodly behaviors that may naturally come forth in a difficult set of circumstances and choose to respond in a Christ-like manner. How is a believer able to do this? What results?

6.  Read James 1:22. Believers are told to be doers of the Word and not hearers only. How does a person deceive himself in this area? Explain the deception.

7.  Let's look deeper at man's deception and how it can impact their faith. Read Matthew 7:21–27 and answer the following questions:

    a.  What two types of people are being addressed in verses 21–23?

    b.  What is the separating quality of these two types of people? (v.21)

c. Why was one group of people deceived? (v.22–23)

## JESUS' EXAMPLE

*In Matthew 23:27–28 Jesus spoke out against the scribes and Pharisees when He spoke about them as being like whitewashed tombs. They looked good on the outside because they were pious and righteous (like being a hearer) but were full of dead men's bones on the inside (like not being a doer). They led others astray from the truth of God by their behaviors. May we not be hypocritical too. When we hear the truth, we need to live the truth!*

8. Read James 1:23–24. Describe why a man peering into a mirror is a good analogy of some one who is a hearer but not a doer.

   a. Read 2 Corinthians 3:18. What do we behold in a mirror? How should it transform us?

   b. If we look too quickly into the "mirror," what may result?

## DEEPER EXPERIENCE

*"When the child of God looks into the Word of God (the glass, the mirror), he sees the Son of God and he is transformed by the Spirit of God to share in the glory of God!" (Warren Weirsbe, Be Mature, p. 65)*

9.  Read James 1:25. The "perfect law of liberty" is the Word of God. Look at the verbs used to describe the person who looks in the mirror in verses 23–24. Now look at the verbs used to describe the person who looks into the law of liberty in verse 25. List the verbs used to describe these two groups.

Verses 23–24 person                    Verse 25 person

    a.  Why is the Word of God and our reaction to it so important in the life of the believer?

10.  Read James 1:26. The word *religious* in this verse means external observances of divine service (Strong's G2357). How do the actions of a religious person show possible deception? What does James say about this person's religion?

11.  In James 1:27 another religious person is described. How is this person different from the one in verse 26?

a. What are the marks of true religion?

b. From this verse, how are the marks of true religion both internal and external? Why is this distinction made?

12. It is interesting that James ends this chapter on trials by addressing the believers' response to the orphan and widow. Why do you think he reminded his audience about these two groups of people who also face difficult trials?

13. Read John 13:34–35. What is one practical way that we show we are doers of the Word? Why is this so vital to our faith?

14. Summarize what you learned about the Word of God's impact on your life in the midst of trials.

## JESUS' EXAMPLE

*In Luke 7:11–17 Jesus witnessed the funeral procession of the only son of a widow. Jesus was moved with compassion and spoke to the woman saying, "Do not weep." Then Jesus put his hand upon the son in the open coffin and told him to rise up. The young man sat up, began to speak, and Jesus presented him to his mother. This miraculous event demonstrates Jesus' heart toward all widows. He has a heart full of mercy toward them and encourages us to have compassion upon them too.*

## ACTING ON GOD'S WORD

James connects our faith in Jesus with obedience. Obedience to the Word of God confirms our belief. There is a tendency to read or hear God's Word and not do anything with it. James called this useless religion. The truths in God's Word will lead us to the heart of God and salvation in Jesus Christ. The Bible is foundational to our faith as well as God's book of instruction for those who believe in Him. Pastor Chris Swansen referenced the word *Bible* as the following acronym, "**B**asic **I**nstruction **B**efore **L**eaving **E**arth." It not only strengthens and grows our faith, but through its power we are transformed into the likeness of Christ. As James said, we look into it like a mirror. We see God's heart, and it changes us so that we can act on what we see. We become doers of the Word, not just women who hear something and then forget what they hear. Let's put into practice what James said. You've looked into God's Word, now what have you learned? What is God asking you to put into practice as you walk out your faith?

**HEAD** | What do I know?

1. Is there anything you learned about God from James 1:19–27?

2. Is there anything you learned about being a doer of the Word and not just being a hearer?

**HEART**   How is God moving in my heart?

1. How did God encourage you from James 1:19–27?

2. Is God exposing any sin in your life as you studied these verses? Identify that sin. What is He asking you to do?

3. How have you been prompted to pray? Write your prayer to the Lord below.

**HABIT**   How is God asking me to live out my faith?

1. Do you desire God's Word each day? If yes, how has it changed you? If no, what keeps you from reading your Bible and pursuing God?

2. How does your faith affect the ways you care for other people? Do you have tenderness toward helping orphans and widows? If so, how do you minister to them? If not, what might you do to care for these precious people?

3. Are you motivated to keep yourself unspotted from the world? How does your love for Jesus affect your motivations?

4. What is one thing you can do this week to apply what you learned from James 1:19–27?

## DELIGHTING IN GOD'S WORD

As you end this week's lesson, write down a verse that God has impressed upon your heart throughout the week and pray it back to the Lord.

Teaching Title _____

_____

_____

_____

_____

_____

_____

_____

_____

_____

_____

_____

_____

_____

_____

_____

_____

_____

_____

_____

_____

_____

Teaching Videos and handouts are available for free at www.delightinginthelord.com.

Teaching Title _____

_____

_____

_____

_____

_____

_____

_____

_____

_____

_____

_____

_____

_____

_____

_____

_____

_____

_____

_____

_____

_____

Teaching Videos and handouts are available for free at www.delightinginthelord.com.

# WEEK 4
# A Faith that Shows no Partiality

As a pastor of a small-town church, located in the mountains of Pennsylvania, life was predictable and happy. The congregants were honest, God-fearing, and generous. They were hardworking and invested themselves in farming and coal as a means to provide for their families. It was not uncommon to find offerings given to the church in the form of eggs, butter, or canned goods. Life as a country pastor was quintessential; it was easy to admire the men and women God had placed in his life and it would have been easy to stay in Philipsburg.

However, when David Wilkerson heard the voice of the Holy Spirit instructing him to go to New York City, he made the choice to leave his comfortable life to obey the Lord's directive. Despite the life he had in Philipsburg, when he heard the Lord telling him to go to New York City he didn't hesitate. In Wilkerson's book, *The Cross and the Switchblade*, he describes how he felt unsuited and ignorant in the sprawling city, yet he could not shake the growing desire to help teens involved in gangs encounter Christ.

During David's second trip to NYC, the Lord orchestrated events that led him to spend time with a gang called the GGI's (Grand Gangsters, Incorporated). As he was led to their clubroom, the path was littered with vodka bottles and garbage. Thin, dirty cats with stiff, sticky fur yowled at him. His guide eventually came to an unmarked door and rapped on it with a series of knocks indicating she was a gang member. As the door swung open, an ill-smelling odor struck his nose. The young woman who answered the door wore a provocative dress, had no shoes, was holding a can of beer, and was smoking a cigarette. She stepped aside to allow David and his guide to enter a dank, dark room full of teenagers. David noticed the depravity of the situation, but he did not judge the occupants unworthy of the gospel; instead, he saw a perfect opportunity to share the simple message of God's love for them. Jesus loved the young people in NYC as much as the farmers in Pennsylvania. There was no room for biases, racism, or ethnic superiority. All people are level at the cross of Christ.

> JESUS NEVER DEMONSTRATED PARTIALITY, AND NEITHER SHOULD A BELIEVER IN HIM.

David's first encounter in a basement clubhouse with the GGI's began his work with teens in New York. He ministered without judgment or partiality, and he led countless people, through love and compassion, into a personal relationship with Jesus Christ.

At the time James was writing his letter to the churches, favoritism was occurring in their meetings. Jesus never demonstrated partiality, and neither should a believer in Him. James wrote to address how everyone should be treated, regardless of their socioeconomic status. Showing partiality to the rich while treating the poor as if they were inferior was a sinful behavior then and still is today!

Jesus taught we should love our neighbor as ourselves and He has no tolerance for favoritism. Christ came to make it possible for all people, whether rich or poor, Jew or Gentile, male or female (Galatians 3:28), to be forgiven and have eternal life. In the church we should be the reflection of this message and be impartial to all by extending grace and mercy to everyone around us. The sin of partiality is often overlooked within the church, but this should not be the case. As we study James chapter 2, may the Lord heighten our awareness regarding any biases we may demonstrate toward the rich or the poor.

## RECEIVING GOD'S WORD

**Open in Prayer**
Read James 2:1–13

## EXPERIENCING GOD'S WORD

### EXPERIENCE 1: A WARNING ABOUT A FAITH THAT FAVORS

1.  Read James 2:1–4 and answer the following questions:

    a.  What warning is given in verse 1 about our faith?

    b.  The word *partiality* has the connotation of respecting one person over another based on their position, rank, circumstance, or popularity. What synonyms would you give for the word *partiality*?

    c.  In verses 2–3 there are two men who came into a gathering of believers. Who received more attention and why?

    d.  How were these men separated? (v.3)

e. What sin did James call out? (v.4)

f. Describe how partiality is really a form of judgment against another person.

g. Verse 4 says that judgment came with evil thoughts. List some possible evil thoughts that accompany this kind of judgment.

2. Read Matthew 7:1–5. What do you learn about judging others from these verses?

a. What are people called who judge others for the very sin they also commit? (v.5)

b. What instructions does Jesus give to the person who is judging another? (v.5)

3. Read Philippians 2:2–4. How should we treat all people according to these verses?

4. What are some ways believers today show partiality within the body of Christ?

## JESUS' EXAMPLE

*"When the Lord Jesus came into the world, He wasn't a rich man's boy; He wasn't born with a silver spoon in His mouth. He was born in poverty. He was born in a borrowed stable. He had to borrow loaves and fishes from a little lad to feed the crowd. He spoke from a borrowed boat. He said, 'The foxes have holes, and the birds of the air have nests; but the Son of man hath not where to lay his head' (Matthew 8:20). He had to borrow a coin to illustrate a truth. He borrowed a donkey to ride into Jerusalem. He borrowed a room to celebrate the Passover. He died on a borrowed cross—it belonged to Barabbas, not to Him. They put Him in a borrowed tomb—it belonged to Joseph of Arimathea." (J. Vernon McGee, Through the Bible Commentary Series, The Epistles: James, p. 53–54)*

5. Read James 2:5–7. This is the fourth time James refers to his readers as "brethren" or "beloved brethren." James uses this term of endearment as he calls out their sinful behavior by speaking the truth in love. James calls into question three behaviors. What are they?

a. How does God describe the person who loves Him in verse 5?

b. The word *oppress* in verse 6 of the NKJV suggests that one person is exercising power over another person. How are the rich in wealth exercising power over others?

## DEEPER EXPERIENCE

*"When we choose people by what we can see on the surface, we miss the mind of God. Remember that Judas appeared to be much better leadership material than Peter." (David Guzik, Enduringword.com on blueletterbible.org)*

6. Read 1 Corinthians 1:26–29. Contrast God's thinking toward people with the world's thinking toward people.

7. Read James 2:8 and Leviticus 19:17–18. In the Old Testament Moses recorded the laws that God gave him regarding how the Israelites should live. What is the royal law found here in James 2:8? How does it reflect the law found in Leviticus?

a. Explain how the royal law commands believers to love others without condition.

## JESUS' EXAMPLE

*In Matthew 22:35–40 a lawyer came to Jesus to test Him and asked, "Teacher, which is the greatest commandment in the law?" Jesus said to Him, "You shall love the LORD your God with all your heart, with all your soul, and with all your mind." Then Jesus went on to say that although this was the first and greatest commandment, the second was like it which was, "You shall love your neighbor as yourself. On these two commandments hang all the Law and the Prophets." Jesus wanted the lawyer and everyone else listening to know that loving your neighbor demonstrated that we also love the Lord our God. It was an action step which demonstrated their faith.*

8. Read James 2:8b–9. How does obedience to this law bring blessing? How does disobedience to this law bring conviction?

9. Read James 2:10–11. Sometimes we tend to think that one sin is more grievous than another. What does James point out about following all of the law, not just some of it?

10. How should our faith and the law of liberty influence our behavior according to James 2:12?

11. From James 2:13, how do mercy and judgment go together?

12. Summarize what you learned about a faith that shows no partiality.

## ACTING ON GOD'S WORD

Our world loves to assign status to people. For example, there is first class seating on an airplane, platinum credit cards, and front row tickets to an event. When someone is given preferential treatment and elevated above others, entitlement and pride can result.

Unfortunately, this does not just happen in the world but can sometimes happen with people who claim they love Christ. James addressed this very problem with his readers and made it clear that the outwardly "rich" people should not be given preferential treatment just because of their appearance and/or status. As the rich were given preferential treatment, the poor were being overlooked. By doing so, they were unjustly judging the very people they were called to serve. Christ came to break down the barriers that divided people and unify them through Himself (Ephesians 2:14–15). With this in mind, we also have an obligation to examine if we are demonstrating preferential treatment toward anyone or judging them based on wealth.

**HEAD** | What do I know?

1. Is there anything you learned about God and what the Bible says about partiality? 1 Samuel 16:7 says, "The LORD does not see as man sees; for man looks at the outward appearance, but the LORD looks at the heart." What have you learned about outward appearances from James 2 and God's heart toward judging others?

**HEART** | How is God moving in my heart?

1. How did God encourage you from James 2:1–13?

2. Is God exposing any sin in your life as you studied these verses? There are several sins we can link to the text, such as selfishness, partiality, favoritism, pride, and love of money. Is God asking you to take a look at any sinful behavior(s) and do something about it? If so, what is He asking you to do?

3. How have you been prompted to pray? Write your prayer to the Lord below.

| HABIT | How is God asking me to live out my faith? |

1. Can you think of an example where you often find yourself tempted to treat one person better than another? Explain what happens when this occurs and describe how you can be on guard against it in the future.

2. Do you need to apologize to anyone you have treated with partiality? If so, when and how will you reach out to that person?

3. If favoritism has crept into your home, friendships, and/or family, how should you address this problem and work toward change?

## DELIGHTING IN GOD'S WORD

As you end this week's lesson, write down a verse that God has impressed upon your heart throughout the week and pray it back to the Lord.

Teaching Title _____

_____

_____

_____

_____

_____

_____

_____

_____

_____

_____

_____

_____

_____

_____

_____

_____

_____

_____

_____

_____

_____

_____

_____

_____

Teaching Videos and handouts are available for free at www.delightinginthelord.com.

Teaching Title _____

_____

_____

_____

_____

_____

_____

_____

_____

_____

_____

_____

_____

_____

_____

_____

_____

_____

_____

_____

_____

_____

_____

Teaching Videos and handouts are available for free at www.delightinginthelord.com.

# WEEK 5
# A FAITH WITHOUT WORKS IS DEAD

They became fast friends during Janet's sophomore year of college. Even though a year separated them, their love for music as well as social interests quickly formed a bond. Being music majors, Anna's and Janet's paths crossed regularly. They spent a significant amount of time together in the classroom as well as parties throughout the week. Despite a busy college schedule, Janet enjoyed her social downtime with drinks and friends.

Towards the end of Janet's sophomore year, her friendship with Anna began to change. Anna was different. Janet couldn't quite pinpoint the change, but Anna wasn't interested in doing the things they previously did on the weekends. Janet didn't probe. One day Anna invited Janet to a Cru (Campus Crusade for Christ) meeting that met on their college campus. Many of the music majors attended the Cru meetings, so Janet went along. Something was stirred in Janet's heart as the conversation turned toward Jesus.

Growing up Catholic, Janet always considered herself a faithful and religious person. She believed in God. She even regularly attended Sunday Mass while away at school because she knew it was the right thing to do. She was what people would call a "good person" who tried to help others. And yet, the meetings she now attended were different from anything she had heard before.

When the Cru music majors decided to start a Bible study, Janet attended. Every Monday night the group met in the university library to read and discussed the Bible. Janet looked forward to the meetings each week. She was learning so much, but when the semester ended so did the meetings. It was during the beginning of her junior year when she hit a spiritual breaking point. While sitting in a Cru meeting, she knew God was asking her to come to Him, repent of her sin, and receive His forgiveness. Janet made a decision to accept Jesus as her Lord and Savior.

> OUR FAITH IN JESUS MUST BE A FAITH THAT IS PROVEN BY OUR WORKS WHICH OVERFLOW FROM A HEART SURRENDERED TO JESUS.

Janet's life slowly began to change. As she saw her friend Anna reading her Bible regularly, Janet followed her example. Janet would arrive on campus early each day and have time with God in His Word. She was growing in God's truths daily. She continued attending the Catholic church on campus as that was familiar to her. One Sunday, during Mass, the priest shared a sermon on tithing. Janet's heart was pricked again as the verses being shared challenged her in a new way. What was God saying about giving back to Him? What was He asking her to do?

That semester her workload was the heaviest it had ever been. She carried 21 credit hours at school while being a part of the university marching band. She taught another marching band 45 minutes from campus and worked four hours a week at Kohls. Her bi-weekly paycheck was just $120, and her expenses were close to that amount. But as she heard Scripture about tithing, God began to speak to her heart. Could she give God from the meager amount of her paycheck?

Her faith said yes. She wrote a check trusting God to provide, and He did. It seemed like a small act of obedience, yet her actions proved her faith. This was her first step of obedience to God, and yet from that day forward she has trusted God in all areas of her life—from finances to family and everything in between. God always rewards obedience even when we, like Janet, do not know the outcome. Janet's giving was the first big step in her faith walk. It wasn't about giving her resources back to God that was most important but rather learning to trust God with the money He would provide for her.

In James 2:14–26 James will examine true, saving faith by explaining what it is and what it isn't. He will use examples of how faith and works must go together. Our faith in Jesus must be a faith that is proven by our works which overflow from a heart surrendered to Jesus. Faith and works are not mutually exclusive. They go together when a genuine, saving faith is present in a person's life. As James will point out, a faith-filled life obeys God and proves itself by its actions, whether small or large, seen or unseen. Like Janet, as God pricks our hearts, may we respond in obedience to Him out of a heart of faith. May our lives show others the love of the Lord by all that we do.

## RECEIVING GOD'S WORD

**Open in Prayer**

Read James 2:14–26

## EXPERIENCING GOD'S WORD

### EXPERIENCE 1: FAITH—DEAD OR ALIVE?

James 2:14–19

1. Read James 2:14. Two questions are being asked in this verse. The word *faith* is used two times as well. The second usage of the word *faith* refers back to the faith James described in the first half of the verse. Summarize what James is saying about faith, works, and salvation.

2. Read James 2:14–16. The word *profit* is in verses 14 and 16. How should our faith be profitable?

3. Read James 2:15–17. In last week's lesson we looked at the royal law in James 2:8 which says, "You shall love your neighbor as yourself." How is the royal law not being fulfilled in verses 15–16?

4. The word *faith* can have a vague meaning. There can be many definitions of faith based on personal opinion, religious teachings, what the world says, and what God says in the Bible. We will use James 2 along with some other verses to find out what the Bible says, but before we do, let's first consider how others define faith. How might faith be defined by each group below?

General definition:

The world's teaching:

Church tradition/religious instruction:

5. Let's look at the Biblical definition of faith. Read Hebrews 11:1–3. How is faith described?

6. Read John 14:6 and John 3:16. Who must be the substance of our faith? What does this kind of faith yield?

7. Read Romans 10:8–13. Describe faith from these verses. How does this kind of faith lead to salvation?

8. Read James 2:17. How is faith which is not a Biblical saving faith described? What synonyms can be used for this description?

9. Read James 2:17. James makes it very clear that there is a correlation between faith and works. Look at the word *have* in verse 17. Saving faith possesses something. What is it? How does one validate the other?

## JESUS' EXAMPLE

*In Matthew 25:34–40 Jesus spoke to His disciples about those who had put their faith in Him. Notice that those who were saved also did good works. Jesus said this, "Then the King will say to those on His right hand, 'Come, you blessed of My Father, inherit the kingdom prepared for you from the foundation of the world: for I was hungry and you gave Me food; I was thirsty and you gave Me drink; I was a stranger and you took Me in; I was naked and you clothed Me; I was sick and you visited Me; I was in prison and you came to Me.' Then the righteous will answer Him, saying, 'Lord, when did we see You hungry and feed You, or thirsty and give You drink? When did we see You a stranger and take You in, or naked and clothe You? Or when did we see You sick, or in prison, and come to You?' And the King will answer and say to them, 'Assuredly, I say to you, inasmuch as you did it to one of the least of these My brethren, you did it to Me.'"*

10. Read Ephesians 2:4–10 and answer the following questions about faith and works:

   a. What did Christ do for the sinner? (v.4–7)

   b. How is the sinner saved? (v.8)

   c. How is salvation NOT obtained? Why? (v.9)

   d. What is one of the reasons we were created? (v.10)

   e. Before God can work through you, He must work in you. Summarize how these verses support this statement by listing what Jesus did for the sinner. (v. 4–10)

## DEEPER EXPERIENCE

*"James did not contradict the Apostle Paul, who insisted that we are saved not of works (Ephesians 2:9, Titus 3:8). James merely clarifies for us the kind of faith that saves. We are saved by grace through faith, not by works; but saving faith will have works that accompany it. As a saying goes: faith alone saves, but the faith that saves is not alone; it has good works with it." (David Guzik, blueletterbible.org)*

11. Read the following verses and note what you learn about faith and works and how they exist together.

John 15:1–5

Colossians 1:10

Titus 3:8

12. Read James 2:18–19. James is contrasting two different kinds of faith. What is the contrast?

13. In verse19 James draws attention to the faith of demons.

    a. What is James saying about the faith of demons and a faith that doesn't produce works?

    b. Read Mark 3:10–11. What do the demons believe about God?

## EXPERIENCE 2: EXAMPLES OF FAITH

James 2:20–26

1. James now illustrates what saving faith looks like. James 2:20 is similar to 2:17. What does James call the man who thinks faith without works is enough? How is faith without works described again?

2. James now uses Abraham to illustrate a saving faith. Read Genesis 22:1–19 and answer the following questions:

   a. What does God ask Abraham to do with Isaac?

   b. How does God intervene?

3. Read James 2:21–24 and answer the following questions:

   a. How does Abraham demonstrate his faith in God? (v.21)

   b. What word is used to show that God accepted Abraham's faith? (v.21)

   c. How was Abraham's faith shown to be a saving faith (perfect/complete)? (v.22)

d. How did Abraham's faith prove he had a genuine relationship with God? (v.23–24)

4. Read James 2:25 for the last illustration of a saving faith. To familiarize yourself with Rahab, read Joshua 2:1–21 and answer the following questions:

   a. What does Rahab declare in Joshua 2:11 about her faith?

   b. What does Rahab do in Joshua 2:21 to demonstrate her faith?

   c. How does James summarize Rahab's saving faith?

5. Read James 2:26. 1 Thessalonians 5:23 tells us that when God created men and women, He gave each person a body, a soul, and a spirit. James makes a comparison between a body without a spirit and faith without works. What is the comparison? What is James' concluding point?

6. Based on what you learned in James 2:14–26, contrast the motivations for works with a saving faith and a works-based faith? How does one bring freedom and the other bondage?

*DEEPER EXPERIENCE*

> *"We will confuse ourselves in seeking to understand what James means by this comparison [of faith and works], if we introduce words describing the relationship between body and spirit: if we say, for example, that the spirit animates the body, and then try to discover how works might be thought to animate faith. We ought to start rather with the fact that unity of body and spirit is required for life, and so also there must be unity of faith and works. They must belong together in a living Christian experience." (J.A. Motyer, The Message of James, p. 110)*

## ACTING ON GOD'S WORD

When a believer has genuine saving faith, their faith will not stand alone; it will be accompanied by good deeds. Just like we would expect cola to come out of a can labeled "Pepsi," works should come forth from a person who claims to be a "Christian." The works which are done prove there is a saving faith present but are never to be confused as a requirement for salvation. The thief on the cross is a good example of this. As we learned, faith is given and received by grace alone (Ephesians 2:8). If there is a saving faith, there should be demonstrable Christ-like behaviors that accompany what the Christian professes. My (Brenda) dad often would ask my brother and me, "If you were put on trial for being a Christian, would there be enough evidence to convict you?" There should be works that accompany our faith. Let's take some time to examine how we are demonstrating our faith in the day-to-day activities of life.

**HEAD** | What do I know?

1. What do you believe about the correlation between faith and works? Have you been taught that each can stand alone?

2. What have you learned from studying James 2:14–26 this week that has challenged or expanded what you believed in the past about faith and works?

**HEART** | **How is God moving in my heart?**

1. How did God encourage you in James 2:14–26?

2. James 2:17 says, "Thus also faith by itself, if it does not have works, is dead." James is saying if we don't demonstrate our faith, we have a lifeless and dead faith. If we have a living faith, we must do something with it. Does this convict you? Why or why not? Explain.

3. How have you been prompted to pray? Write your prayer to the Lord below.

**HABIT** | **How is God asking me to live out my faith?**

1. If you were put on trial for being a Christian in your state's courthouse, would there be enough evidence to convict you? What would the primary evidence be and what does it prove?

2.  How do you tell the difference between works that come from your love for God and works that don't?

3.  When you have sensed God asking you to demonstrate your faith by doing something, how have you responded? Was this easy or difficult? Explain.

4.  When you think of faith and good works being expressed well in someone, is there a person who comes to mind? What is it about their example of good deeds that demonstrates their faith and trust in Christ? Is there something in their example worth following?

## DELIGHTING IN GOD'S WORD

As you end this week's lesson, write down a verse that God has impressed upon your heart throughout the week and pray it back to the Lord.

Teaching Title _____

_____

_____

_____

_____

_____

_____

_____

_____

_____

_____

_____

_____

_____

_____

_____

_____

_____

_____

_____

_____

_____

_____

_____

Teaching Videos and handouts are available for free at www.delightinginthelord.com.

Teaching Title _____

_____

_____

_____

_____

_____

_____

_____

_____

_____

_____

_____

_____

_____

_____

_____

_____

_____

_____

_____

_____

_____

_____

_____

_____

Teaching Videos and handouts are available for free at www.delightinginthelord.com.

# WEEK 6
# A FAITH THAT CONTROLS
# ITS TONGUE

George Müller's financial debt had grown greater than his ability to pay back what he owed to cover his many nights of drinking and gambling. He needed a creative scheme to obtain the money necessary to pay his creditors. He had learned early in his life how to use his words to get what he wanted. Müller became skilled at deception and fabricating intricate lies to solve the trouble he created. Just like he had done in previous situations, George concocted a devious plan to solve his money problem. He decided he would fake a theft in his room, and then take advantage of his good-natured and generous friends who he believed would come to his rescue.

George had always enjoyed the theater, so like a skilled play writer, he crafted lines for his performance. He decided that when the allowance his father sent him arrived, he would make a big fuss about it. Then he would go into his room, hide the money in the false bottom of his trunk, and then smash the lock on the trunk to make it look as though someone had broken into his dorm room and stolen his money.

> OUR WORDS HAVE POWER FOR EITHER LIFE OR DEATH. THEIR INFLUENCE IS FAR REACHING.

The events unfolded exactly as he planned. The other men on his floor came running to his room to examine what had happened, and just as George had anticipated, his friends had empathy upon his situation. They took up a collection for him, and by the time his friends presented him with their donations, there was more than twice the amount of what his dad had initially sent. His plot of deception had worked flawlessly, and instead of being remorseful, he congratulated himself on his ingenious plan of duplicity. His convincing words and actions got him what he wanted and had solved his temporary problem.

However, in the fall of 1825, God interrupted George's life when he agreed to join a friend for a Bible meeting. In just one night, everything changed. He told his friend on their way home, "All we have seen on our journey to Switzerland, and all our former pleasures, are nothing in comparison with this evening." As George prepared for bed, he knelt and asked God to forgive him for all that he had done, and God's grace was extended to him. This prayer became the first of his conversations with God. Prayer would become the secret to his changed life and the way he would make decisions. In the past he would use his deceitful words to get what he needed. After putting his faith in God, his words were used for much better use as bold prayers to God to supply all his needs. His days of deception were over, and his new life of trusting God had begun.

For the next sixty years, George Müller lived a life that was marked by faith in God and the power of prayer. Without ever soliciting for donations or receiving government funding, he established 117 schools which offered Christian education to over 120,000 orphans in England. He simply prayed to God for all of his needs, and God faithfully provided. George often documented his answers to prayer in his journals like this one:

*"One morning, all the plates and cups and bowls on the table were empty. There was no food in the larder and no money to buy food. The children were standing, waiting for their morning meal, when Müller said, 'Children, you know we must be in time for school.' Then lifting up his hands he prayed, 'Dear Father, we thank Thee for what Thou art going to give us to eat.' There was a knock at the door. The baker stood there, and said, 'Mr. Müller, I couldn't sleep last night. Somehow, I felt you didn't have bread for breakfast, and the Lord wanted me to send you some. So, I got up at 2 a.m. and baked some fresh bread and have brought it.' Mr. Müller thanked the baker, and no sooner had he left, when there was a second knock at the door. It was the milkman. He announced that his milk cart had broken down right in front of the orphanage, and he would like to give the children his cans of fresh milk so he could empty his wagon and repair it. "*

Over the course of his life, George learned not to use his words for selfish gain but instead to turn them into prayers to an all-powerful God. His words reflected his faith. His life came under the authority and power of God, and his tongue followed. James wrote, "No man can tame the tongue. It is an unruly evil, full of deadly poison." (James 3:8). This is a true statement, but there is One who can tame our tongue, the Lord Jesus Christ. Just as George Müller's words were affected once he put his faith in God, so too our words can be bridled when the Holy Spirit is ruling within us. George said less and prayed more. He didn't use his intellect to devise schemes but trusted and waited silently on the Lord to help him.

Our words have power for either life or death. Their influence is far reaching. We must take the warning seriously that James gives us about the tongue in chapter 3 and learn to control what is spoken and unspoken. This cannot be done in our own strength; however, it is possible through the power of the Holy Spirit. George Müller's life reminds us that anyone can change when they submit their life to God's authority and learn to pray more and speak less.

## RECEIVING GOD'S WORD

**Open in Prayer**
Read James 3:1–12

## EXPERIENCING GOD'S WORD

### EXPERIENCE 1: A BRIDLED WORD

James 3:1–5a

1.  James begins chapter 3 with a caution. Read James 3:1. What warning is given? Why?

2.  Think about teachers for a moment. Describe the primary role of a teacher and how they accomplish their duties. Why might James have singled out this group of people?

3.  The Greek word for *teacher* is *didaskalos* (Strong's G1320). It can be translated as *master*. The word is often used as a title for Jesus Christ. In the New Testament the word refers to one who teaches the things of God and the duties of man. Read Matthew 23:1–8. What point was Jesus making about teachers as He spoke to the Pharisees?

    a.  According to James 3:1 why should they be concerned about what Jesus said in Matthew 23:1–8?

4.  Read James 3:2. What does James say about all people, including himself? What area of stumbling does James specifically address?

a. The word *perfect* is used in verse 2. That word is *teleios* (Strong's G5046) in the Greek. It means to be complete in moral character. From this verse, describe the perfect man and what he is able to do. Who is the only one who is perfect?

b. Why would James link the control of the mouth to the whole body in verse 2?

5. Explain the connection you see between verses 1 & 2 regarding teachers. Why would James start with talking about teachers while exhorting believers about the control over their words?

## DEEPER EXPERIENCE

*"Surely James wrote that ['he is a perfect man' 3:2] as his personal tribute to the Lord Jesus. That wondrous Person had lived with him in the same home in Nazareth for many years. He had attended the same school and synagogue and had worked beside Him at the carpenter's bench. Then, for three and one-half years, He had traversed the length and breadth of the Promised Land teaching, encouraging, debating, rebuking and warning. How well James knew it. He and Jesus had grown up together. Looking back on that experience, James pondered the significance of it all. He had never heard Him say anything suggestive or vulgar or say anything of which afterward, He would have felt ashamed. He had never heard him speak angrily in a fit of temper or say anything that called for an apology. On the contrary, everything that Jesus ever said had been wise, loving, kind and true. Looking back over the Nazareth years, James could think of no better definition of perfection: 'The man who can claim that he never says anything wrong is perfect!' Jesus was perfect. His control of His tongue demonstrates the fact." (John Philips, Exploring the Epistle of James: An Expository Commentary, p. 97)*

6. Read James 3:3–5 and answer the following questions:

    a. Describe the two analogies James gives in these verses.

    b. How do these analogies incorporate submission in their description?

    c. Consider size and force/pressure in these two analogies. What do you notice?

7. Look up the following verses about a bridled tongue and note what you learn.

Proverbs 11:13

Proverbs 13:3

Matthew 5:37

1 Peter 3:10

## JESUS' EXAMPLE

*Jesus stood bloody and beaten before Pilate. The chief priests and elders falsely accused Him, yet "He answered nothing." (Matthew 27:12). Pilate said to Jesus, "Do you not hear how many things they testify against You?" Jesus said nothing in return. This caused Pilate to marvel greatly. Jesus stood silent, not because He was afraid to speak but because He was able to perfectly bridle his tongue and His entire body in the midst of dire circumstances.*

## EXPERIENCE 2: A POWERFUL WORD

James 3:5b–8

1. Read James 3:5b–6 and answer the following questions:

   a. Explain what the tongue is being compared to in these verses. What is the similarity? (v. 5b–6)

   b. How is the tongue described? (v. 6)

   c. What/who sparks the fire of the tongue? (v. 6)

2. The tongue has great influence over the body. The word *body* in verse 6 encompasses the whole person, both inward and outward, by describing it as the instrument of life. Considering this definition, what influence does the tongue specifically have on the individual parts of the physical body?

a. James 3:6 says, "…The tongue is so set among our members that it defiles the whole body…" Read 1 Corinthians 12:12–14. Apply what James is saying about the influence our individual tongue has within the body of Christ.

3. The tongue also has influence over nature, as seen in verse 6, by affecting its course over time. The word *nature* is *genesis* (Strong's G1078). It refers to the timespan of life. Explain what James is saying about the tongue's influence on a person's life.

4. Read Proverbs 18:21. How does this proverb summarize James 3:5–8 well?

5. Read James 3:7 and Genesis 1:28. What authority did God give to man? What observation does James make about the animal kingdom and man's influence over it in verse 7?

6. Read James 3:8. Even though man can tame animals, what can man not tame in his/her own strength? Does this mean it is untamable overall? Explain.

7. James 3:8 can seem like a defeated statement on its own. Read Galatians 5:16–17. What hope does this verse give us about taming the tongue?

8. God gives us the ability to tame our tongues. Look up the following verses and note how this is possible.

   Romans 8:9

   Galatians 2:19–20

   Galatians 5:22–23

9. What destructive words are used in James 3:8b to describe the tongue and its power?

10. Read Ephesians 4:29–32. How are these verses an encouragement regarding the problem identified in verse 8b?

## EXPERIENCE 3: AN INCONSISTENT WORD

James 3:9–12

1. Read James 3:9. An inconsistency is given about our words. What is this inconsistency?

2. When words are formed, they can be spoken or unspoken. Anything that is produced in thought, mental pictures, emotions, or comes forth as oral language is a result of words and the tongue. With this in mind, how might our words bless God? Give an example(s).

   a. How do our words curse men? Give an example(s).

3. Read James 3:9 and Genesis 1:26–27. How is man described according to these verses?

   a. When we either think or speak about another person in an unloving way, who are we actually cursing/insulting? Explain how.

4. Read James 3:10. James makes a plea to believers regarding our faith and words. Why is it inconsistent for a believer to behave the way James describes people in this verse? How might this damage the testimony of a Christian before others?

5. Read James 3:11–12 and Genesis 1:11–12, 24–25. What order did God bring to creation?

   a. What inconsistency is seen in James 3:11–12?

   b. Based on God's order and James' analogy, what consistency should be seen in the life of the believer regarding our thoughts and words?

6. Jesus spoke about people and their words in the Gospels. Let's see what he says. Read Matthew 12:33–35 and answer the following questions:

   a. How is a tree known? (v. 33)

b. What inconsistency was Jesus pointing out? (v. 33–34)

c. What does it mean when Jesus says, "Out of the abundance of the heart the mouth speaks?" (v. 34)

d. Based on what Jesus said in these verses, how do His words give a similar message to the one James wrote in James 3:11–12?

7. Summarize what you learned about a faith that controls its tongue.

## DEEPER EXPERIENCE

"James does not simply say that the tongue is untamable, but that it cannot be subdued by any power resident in mere human nature or possessed by a mere human being. Beyond this he does not go, but he may feel that the hint is plain enough. On the day of Pentecost (Acts 2:2–4) a different fire from that which ascends from Gehenna descended from heaven to kindle new powers and give new speech to the human tongue. If we must say that the outworking of sin first appeared in the abuse of speech (Genesis 3:12), we must also say that the first act in the new creation was the renewal of the power of speech, a tongue intelligibly declaring the wonderful works of God (Acts 2:11)". (J.A. Motyer, The Message of James, pg. 124–125).

## ACTING ON GOD'S WORD

In a 2007 study done at the University of Arizona, it was found that men and women speak about 16,000 words a day. Women speak a little more, and men speak a little less. That number only reflects what comes out of the average person's mouth. It doesn't account for the unspoken words that formulate through thought, mental planning, writing, and images. That's a lot of words in 24 hours that are all connected to our tongues.

As we learned in James 3:1–12, "The tongue is a little member and boasts great things." Day in and day out, the tongue speaks. We are accountable for what our tongue says and its influence over the receiver of each word. The question we must ask is, "Who is controlling my words?" Do I speak under the power of the Holy Spirit as I submit my life to Christ, or do I speak under the power of my flesh and selfishness?

As we saw in this lesson, what we speak is an indicator of our faith and walk with Jesus. What comes out of our mouth is a gauge of what is within the depths of our soul, body, and spiritual state. Its influence is pervasive. Our words tell a story to others that goes much deeper than what is actually said (or not said) from our mouth. In short, our words should match our Godly testimony. May we encourage you to stop for a moment and pray this verse to the Lord before you begin the Acting section.

*"Search me, O God, and know my heart; Try me, and know my anxieties; And see if there is any wicked way in me, And lead me in the way everlasting." Psalm 139:23–24*

| **HEAD** | What do I know? |

1. Is there anything you learned about God and His desire for you regarding your spoken and unspoken words?

2. What did you learn about the power of the tongue and how it can be controlled?

**HEART** How is God moving in my heart?

1. How did God encourage you in James 3:1–12?

2. Did God expose any sin in your life as you studied these verses? Can you identify any sinful roots in your heart that are producing ungodly words or thoughts?

3. Psalm 19:14 says, "Let the words of my mouth and the meditation of my heart be acceptable in Your sight, O LORD, my strength and my Redeemer." Use this verse as a guide to create a prayer back to the Lord based on what you have learned about guarding your tongue. Confess any sin that He has identified in your life.

**HABIT** | **How is God asking me to live out my faith?**

1. Identify any area(s) you struggle with regarding your tongue. Check all that apply.

__ Raising my voice in anger      __ Lying/exaggerating

__ Sarcasm      __ Cursing

__ Judging others      __ Gossip

__ Self-pity/complaining      __ Boasting/prideful

__ Hasty words      __ Lustfulness/greed

__ Bitter words/resentment      __ Unkindness

__ Unloving words      __ Derogatory comments/tone of voice

__ Negativity      __ Belittling words

__ Flattery      __ Other _____

    a. Can you identify any triggers that produce these words in your heart that then overflow from your mouth?

    b. What is one thing you can do today to begin working on this area?

    c. Accountability is often critical when we are trying to make a change. Is there someone you can ask to help hold you accountable to the steps you are making to change? Who is that person?

2. Do you take your ability to influence others with your words for granted? You can either turn people to Christ by bringing peace, gentleness, and wisdom to a relationship or situation, or you can turn people away from God by bringing division, anger, and selfish opinions to a relationship or situation. Before you speak to others ask yourself: Is it true? Is it necessary? Is it kind? Consider a relationship where you have great influence. What steps can you take in this relationship to use your words as a Godly force?

## DELIGHTING IN GOD'S WORD

As you end this week's lesson, write down a verse that God has impressed upon your heart through-out the week and pray it back to the Lord.

Teaching Title _____

_____

_____

_____

_____

_____

_____

_____

_____

_____

_____

_____

_____

_____

_____

_____

_____

_____

_____

_____

Teaching Videos and handouts are available for free at www.delightinginthelord.com.

Teaching Title _____

_____
_____
_____
_____
_____
_____
_____
_____
_____
_____
_____
_____
_____
_____
_____
_____
_____
_____
_____
_____
_____

Teaching Videos and handouts are available for free at www.delightinginthelord.com.

# WEEK 7
# A FAITH THAT DISPLAYS GODLY WISDOM IN RELATIONSHIPS

# WEEK 7: A FAITH THAT DISPLAYS GODLY WISDOM IN RELATIONSHIPS

Conflict, confusion, and alienation defined their mother-daughter relationship. It hadn't always been that way. But the last ten years were different. Prior to this, they disagreed on things and had their occasional fight, but nothing lasted long. However, a deep family trial brought on relational conflict causing silence and estrangement despite attempts at reconciliation and restoration. Despite all her efforts, the silence and hurt remained. As she worked through the pain with the Lord, she decided she could either grow bitter and angry, or give the relationship over to the Lord waiting on Him to bring healing.

Each day since then, she has seen God give her more grace to walk through the pain (James 4:6a) as she sought Him.

As a believer in Christ, she found hope in God alone. She learned to lean on His wisdom, fighting the urge to take matters into her own hands. In the early days of the broken relationship, she sought counsel from other people who were filled with godly wisdom. They helped. But she knew that in Jesus she'd find sustaining power, comfort, and peace to help her navigate the road of pain and conflict. As she desired more of Him and His wisdom, He filled her. As

> IT IS THE PERSON WHO HUMBLY FEARS GOD AND TRUSTS HIM WHO WILL ENJOY ALL THE WISDOM HE OFFERS, ESPECIALLY WHEN EXPERIENCING RELATIONAL CONFLICT.

time continued, God graciously showed her areas of personal sin. Initially she only saw the relationship from her perspective. In doing so, her finger easily pointed at her daughter. However, that wasn't her responsibility. Her responsibility was to look at herself before a righteous, holy God and respond obediently to what He showed her in her heart. She was to trust Him each day with the relationship and wait on Him. In her waiting...

She humbled herself before God as she grieved.
She received more grace.

She poured her heart out to Him in her need and desire for reconciliation.
She received more grace.

She continued to seek Him in His Word for more of His wisdom.
More grace.

With each falling tear, each merciful cry, each act of submission to God,
He gave her more of His grace to help in her pain.

With each passing year of silence, her prayer remains unanswered. And yet, the longer the conflict goes, the deeper God's peace goes as she trusts Him alone to bring restoration one day. It doesn't mean it is easy, but God's grace meets her in the moments of pain as she turns to Him.

In James 3:13–4:10, James will tackle the difficult topic of conflict in relationships. The people he was writing to were experiencing quarrels and slander as well as relational pressures within the church. Our lives are no different. James continues to teach how faith is proven in the way we live our lives, so it goes without saying that relationships must be addressed. As we've seen James do before, he will pose questions to us to challenge what we believe. In this case, it will be in the area of wisdom and the specific effect it has on other people. James will present two types of wisdom. Each type of wisdom produces something; one being conflict and the other peace.

It is the person who humbly fears God and trusts Him who will enjoy all the wisdom He offers, especially when experiencing relational conflict. This is demonstrated in the life of the woman described above who walks in pain yet experiences the peace that only godly wisdom provides. She knows that even though she can't see God's tangible resolution, He is at work, and she is at peace as she waits for Him to bring restoration.

Perhaps you can relate to the pain this woman experiences. You may have or have had broken relationships filled with conflict and misunderstandings. What kind of wisdom are you employing in the relationship? Do you seek God's wisdom or follow the wisdom of this world? As you study these verses, be encouraged that God sees your pain. He desires you to trust Him as you seek His wisdom in difficult relationships.

## RECEIVING GOD'S WORD

**Open in Prayer**
Read James 3:13–4:10

## EXPERIENCING GOD'S WORD

### EXPERIENCE 1: TWO KINDS OF WISDOM—GODLY AND EARTHLY

James 3:13–18

1. Just as James wrote in James 3:12 that a Christian life should be consistent in its actions, we find this same theme continued in James 3:13. Read this verse. How should a wise person prove their wisdom?

2. In verse 13 James is addressing all believers. James is writing to churches in the midst of conflict. Read the verses below and note how godly wisdom is obtained.

   Job 28:28

   Proverbs 1:7

   Proverbs 2:6–7

   Colossians 2:8

3. In James 3:13 James connects the word *meekness* to the word *wisdom*, further emphasizing what wise conduct looks like. Meekness is demonstrated both as an inward posture toward God and an outward grace toward others. It is sometimes used as a synonym for humility. Describe how a person can be both wise and humble (meek).

## JESUS' EXAMPLE

*Several times Jesus is described in the Bible as meek. When speaking to the Jews in Matthew 11:29, He encouraged them to come unto Him for help and rest and said to them, "Take my yoke upon you, and learn of me; for I am meek and lowly in heart: and ye shall find rest unto your souls." (KJV). When Jesus rode into Jerusalem on a donkey on Palm Sunday, Matthew 21:5 quotes the prophet Zechariah saying, "Tell ye the daughter of Sion, behold, thy King cometh unto thee, meek, and sitting upon an ass, and a colt the foal of an ass." Both of these incidents demonstrate that although Jesus had all power and authority given to Him by God, He chose to exhibit meekness.*

## DEEPER EXPERIENCE

*"The phrase 'meekness of wisdom' is an interesting one. Meekness is the right use of power, and wisdom is the right use of knowledge. They go together." (Warren Weirsbe, Be Mature: Growing up in Christ, p. 117)*

4. Read James 3:14–15. James gives a description of earthly wisdom. Describe the characteristics of a person living under this kind of wisdom.

    a. How is earthly wisdom in direct opposition to the truth contained in the Bible?

    b. What do all these behaviors have in common? What appears to be their cause?

    c. According to verse 15 how is earthly wisdom described?

5. Read James 3:16. There is an effect that is produced from following earthly wisdom. Just as we learned that a good tree produces good fruit, a bad tree produces bad fruit. What is the fruit that earthly wisdom yields?

6. Read James 3:17. Now James contrasts earthly wisdom with "wisdom from above" (godly wisdom). There is a progression of attributes given in this verse. List them below.

   a. What do all the attributes have in common?

7. Explain the effect the behaviors described in verses 16–17 have on relationships.

8. Read 1 Corinthians 1:20–25. What do you learn about godly wisdom from these verses that adds to what you already learned?

9. Read 1 Corinthians 2:1–5. Paul was a man filled with godly wisdom. How do his actions prove his wisdom?

10. Read James 3:18. The concept of sowing and reaping is presented. What is being sown and what harvest is being reaped by the person who follows godly wisdom?

    a. Consider fruit that grows on a tree. Is that fruit for the tree's consumption or the consumption of others? Apply this concept to the fruit of righteousness that James is talking about in verse 18.

## DEEPER EXPERIENCE

*"We come now to the central issue James has in mind. We have seen through his eyes our need of a pure source (12). He has outlined his basic position (13–14) that there is a wisdom, working through self-subduing gentleness, productive of a life of lovely goodness; but alternatively, there is sharp, defensive self-concern leading to division and party-spirit, exposing the absence of the truth from the heart. Now he is ready to put the vital choice to us: is the wisdom of earth (15–16) or of heaven (17–18) to rule our lives?"* (J.A. Motyer, The Message of James, pg. 133)

## EXPERIENCE 2: WORLDLY WISDOM'S EFFECT ON RELATIONSHIPS

James 4:1–6

1. What is happening among believers in James 4:1? Why is this occurring?

2. James started verse 3:13 with a question and now asks another one in James 4:1 regarding relationships and our conduct. Is the person described in verse 13 the same person James is talking about in James 4:1? Explain.

3. What is the cause of conflict among people according to James 4:1? How does this conflict not only affect others but also themselves?

4. Read James 4:2 and then fill in the blanks.

   "You _____ and do not have. You _____ and _____ and cannot obtain. You _____ and _____. Yet you do not have because you do not ask." (NKJV)

a. What phrase stands out to you in the previous verse (p.98) through its repetition? Circle the phrase as it is used. Why is this phrase important in understanding the point James is making?

b. Read Exodus 20:12–17 which is the second half of the Ten Commandments. What similarities do you see between God's commandments in Exodus and the behaviors seen in James 4:2?

5. Consider how conflict creates division. From James 4:1–2, who is the enemy in personal conflict? Explain.

## DEEPER EXPERIENCE

"When at last we do attempt to avail ourselves of the privilege of prayer, our petitions are so self-centered and so concerned about the gratification of our own desires that God cannot in faithful-ness grant our requests. True prayer is not asking God to do what we want, but first of all it is asking Him to enable us to do that which He would have us to do. Too often we endeavor by prayer to control God instead of taking the place of submission to His holy will. Thus, we ask and receive not; because if God answered by giving what we desire, we would but consume it on our lusts, or pleasures. To pray aright there must be a separated life, with God Himself." (H.A. Ironside, James and 1 and 2 Peter: An Ironside Expository Commentary, p.34)

6. The people described in James 4:2–3 are defined as adulterers in James 4:4. How do their behaviors resemble that of marital adultery?

a. Read Isaiah 54:5. Who is the husband and how is He described?

b. Who is committing adultery and with whom is it occurring?

c. Read Psalm 37:4. Why is seeking pleasure apart from God like adultery?

7. Read James 4:5. How does God respond to people who exhibit these behaviors? Explain why.

a. Go back to Exodus 20 and read verses 3–7. These commandments encompass our relationship with God. What consistency do you see in God's character from Exodus 20:3–7 and James 4:5?

## JESUS' EXAMPLE

*One day Jesus shared a parable. In His parable He told the story of two men who went to the temple to pray. One man was a Pharisee and the other was a tax collector. These groups of people were often at odds with each other. The Pharisee, who was considered part of the Jewish religious elite, spoke for all to hear as he prayed. He thanked God that he wasn't like other men; the extortioners, unjust, adulterers, or even like a tax collector. He loudly proclaimed all the good, religious things he had done. The tax collector, on the other hand, bowed his head, beat his chest, and cried out to God asking for mercy on his sinful heart. As Jesus finished the parable, he told those around him that He will humble those who pridefully exalt themselves and He will exalt those who humble themselves before Him. He made it clear that to trust in yourself is pride and to trust in God shows humility. It was the humble man who God justified (Luke 18:9–14).*

8. Read Proverbs 6:16–19. How do these verses correlate to what James says in James 4:4–5?

9. Read James 4:6. James is quoting this verse from Proverbs 3:34. In James 4:6 the word *resists* is *antitassō* (Strong's G498). It means to oppose oneself; to battle. Vines Bible Dictionary describes this word as a military term which means to battle against. Consider this definition in James 4:6 regarding God's reaction to the proud. Rewrite James 4:6 below replacing "resists" with "battles against."

God _____ the proud.

a. Why does God identify pride as the quality that He resists? If you need some help with this question, use these verses: Isaiah 14:12–15, Psalm 10:4, Proverbs 16:18.

10. How does pride both hinder a relationship with God as well as other people?

11. Read James 4:6. What does God want to give a humble believer?

12. Read Hebrews 12:14–15. How do the instructions of this verse summarize James 3:18 and James 4:6 well?

## EXPERIENCE 3: GODLY WISDOM IN ACTION

Read James 4:7–10

1. James gives eight commands for combating worldly wisdom in James 4:7–10. Remember, James is addressing wars and fights among people. In the chart below, we've listed the commands. Fill in the chart by explaining how the flesh and worldly wisdom oppose these commands.

| James 4:7–10 Commands | How does the flesh respond in opposition to these commands? |
| --- | --- |
| 1. Submit to God (v.7) | |
| 2. Resist the devil (v.7) | |
| 3. Draw near to God (v.8) | |
| 4. Cleanse your hands (v.8) | |
| 5. Purify your hearts (v.8) | |
| 6. Lament, and mourn, and weep (v.9) | |
| 7. Let your laughter be turned to mourning and your joy to gloom (v.9) | |
| 8. Humble yourselves in the sight of the Lord (v.10) | |

2. What godly characteristic is needed to follow these commands? Do you see a commonality woven through all of them? Explain.

3. Summarize what you learned about a faith that displays Godly wisdom in relationships.

## ACTING ON GOD'S WORD

James was concerned about relationships and the dissension that was occurring. People were arguing and selfishly pursuing their own desires. James' words are strong and straightforward in our text this week. He sharply contrasts the two kinds of wisdom which exist: earthly wisdom and godly wisdom. James wants his readers to examine themselves and question their motives to determine if they are following their flesh or God's Holy Spirit regarding their interactions with others.

We learned that when we follow worldly wisdom, conflict often occurs. At the heart of all war, fights, strife, and broken relationships is selfishness. It is part of the demonic realm (James 3:15). When we as believers get caught up in worldly wisdom and follow our flesh, the enemy is thrilled with what results in relationships. Evil deeds and confusion are hallmark traits connected to him, and when we see them, it should be a red warning flag to us. We need to take a step back and ask some questions before moving ahead with our actions. Let's be careful when conflict arises. Think before we speak and pray before we act.

**HEAD** | What do I know?

1. Is there anything you learned about God and His desire for you regarding wisdom in relationships?

2. Is there anything you learned about godly wisdom and earthly wisdom that has caused you to consider the wisdom you most frequently follow?

**HEART**   **How is God moving in my heart?**

1. How did God encourage you from James 3:13–4:10?

2. Is God exposing any sin in your life as you studied these verses?

3. Can you identify any selfish or prideful thoughts or actions which are damaging any of your relationships? List them and then pray and ask God for forgiveness.

**HABIT** | **How is God asking me to live out my faith?**

1. Identify a relationship in your life that challenges you to respond with godly wisdom. Why does this relationship challenge you? How can you apply James' teaching to your relational situation?

2. James 3:18 says, "Now the fruit of righteousness is sown in peace by those who make peace." How can you sow peace this week in a difficult relationship?

## DELIGHTING IN GOD'S WORD

As you end this week's lesson, write down a verse that God has impressed upon your heart throughout the week and pray it back to the Lord.

Teaching Title _____

_____

_____

_____

_____

_____

_____

_____

_____

_____

_____

_____

_____

_____

_____

_____

_____

_____

_____

_____

_____

_____

_____

Teaching Videos and handouts are available for free at www.delightinginthelord.com.

Teaching Title _____

_____

_____

_____

_____

_____

_____

_____

_____

_____

_____

_____

_____

_____

_____

_____

_____

_____

_____

_____

_____

Teaching Videos and handouts are available for free at www.delightinginthelord.com.

# WEEK 8
# A FAITH THAT TRUSTS GOD

She had been an elementary school teacher for years. It was actually her career that brought her to her husband on a military base in Turkey. They had been married for ten years with two vibrant daughters, ages 7 and 3, and another one on the way. Life was full and seemingly idyllic despite some challenging marital undercurrents. When they learned that their family of four was expanding to five, her husband decided they needed to move. The house in the village would quickly be outgrown. Building plans had been in place for months to move up the hill to a bigger house just outside the village. Even though she wasn't thrilled about the move, she tried to embrace it.

But everything changed in a moment's notice. She had some weird symptoms leading up to that awful day but had shrugged them off as pregnancy related. No one was prepared for what happened to her in November 1975.

Life forever changed.

She had a massive brain aneurysm. A few weeks away from her baby's due date, the baby had to be quickly delivered so doctors could turn their attention to the swelling

> WHEN WE AREN'T TRUSTING GOD, WE OFTEN TAKE MATTERS INTO OUR OWN HANDS, ACTING INDEPENDENTLY FROM GOD.

that was happening in her brain. It was all a blur. Multiple brain surgeries were needed, months in the hospital, and weeks in rehab. With the left side of her body paralyzed from the aneurysm, she was confined to a wheelchair as the doctors said she'd probably never walk again. For six months, all she had seen were the four walls of her hospital room. Her old house was just a memory along with the life she lived just months before.

Having been discharged from the hospital, her husband was now rolling her through the doorway into their new house. What should have been an exciting entrance was mixed with anxiety, fears, and unknowns. It was the first time she would be seeing the house. How would she adapt? How would she take care of three small children from a wheelchair? How would they pay the bills of the new house now that she couldn't work? How could this possibly be the life that God had for her?

She had always been a woman of saving faith in Jesus Christ, but she wasn't a stranger to hardship. She had learned how to trust God again and again in her circumstances since she was a young, orphaned girl. But this trial touched every aspect of life; challenging not only her trust in God but her emotional responses to her life in a whole new way.

It has been 46 years since that day.

In the years after her aneurysm, God restored her ability to walk despite her paralysis. Much of life remained difficult. She went through a divorce. She raised three girls on her own with her social security and disability checks and learned how to rely on the Lord for everything. She had to learn how to trust God even more deeply with her life, the moments of each day, and all of her finances. Despite it all, she has said again and again, she wouldn't change it. God has been faithful, and her faith built out of pain. The longer she has walked through her circumstances, the more glorious eternity becomes. She knows that one day soon, when she sees Jesus face-to-face, all will be made right. I (Stacy) have had the blessing of witnessing this life of faith as this woman is my mother.

In James 4:11–5:12 James will once again address believers undergoing difficult circumstances in life. So often our hardships can cause us to blame others and say things to get out of our situations as well as create a sense of independence in us, leaving God out. James will deal with all of these heart responses. They boil down to faith. When we aren't trusting God, we often take matters into our own hands, acting independently from God. This section will close with James refocusing all of us to eternity. He will remind us of Christ's return. Be patient; He's coming. As you wait, sweet sister, establish your heart in Him.

## RECEIVING GOD'S WORD

**Open in Prayer**
Read James 4:11–5:12

## EXPERIENCING GOD'S WORD

### EXPERIENCE 1: ENTRUSTING PEOPLE TO GOD

James 4:11–12

1. Read James 4:11. Fill in the blanks.

    Do not _____ _____ of one another, brethren.

    He who _____ _____ of a brother and _____ his brother,

    _____ _____ of the law and _____ the law. But if you

    _____ the law, you are not a doer of the law but a _____. (NKJV)

    a. What relationships are being addressed in this verse? What word(s) are used to give you this understanding?

b. There is a progression that James puts forth in this verse. What is that progression?

2. The word *judge* is *krino* (Strong's G2919), which means to condemn. Explain the gravity of this definition when we use it against another person.

3. Read Leviticus 19:15–18 concerning moral laws given by God to man. What is being commanded in these verses about how we treat our brothers and sisters in the Lord?

   a. How are we speaking evil of the law when we judge others?

4. Read Matthew 7:1–5. What does Jesus say about judging others?

5. Read James 4:12. When we pass judgment on another person, whose place do we assume?

   a. Consider what motivates you to judge another person. What does the judgment of another person actually say about each of us?

6. Read the following verses about God's judgment. How is His judgment perfect?

1 Chronicles 28:9


Revelation 19:11


## EXPERIENCE 2: ENTRUSTING MY DAYS TO GOD

James 4:13–17

1. Read James 4:13–15 and answer the following questions:

   a. James draws attention to the actions of another group of people. What are these people doing? (v.13)




   b. What presumptions are these people making about life? (v.14a)




   c. How does James describe life? (v.14)




   d. How does James exhort them to change? (v.15)

2. Read the following verses and note what you learn about entrusting your days to God.

   Psalm 39:4

   Psalm 90:12

   Psalm 139:16

   Proverbs 19:21

## JESUS' EXAMPLE

*Before Jesus was betrayed and arrested in the Garden of Gethsemane, He spent some time alone in prayer and said, "O, My Father, if it is possible, let this cup pass from Me; nevertheless, not as I will but as You will" (Matthew 26:39). Jesus demonstrates in this verse that He entrusted His days to God; even the most difficult days of His life were under God's direction and authority. As He yielded to God the Father, so should we.*

3. Is James trying to banish planning from a person's life? Explain your answer.

4. Read James 4:16. Why are these people boasting? Why does James call it arrogant and evil?

5. Read James 4:17. Here James calls out sinful behavior. What needs to be repented of? How should they approach life differently?

6. Read Romans 12:1–2. How does this verse help put our life and plans in focus before God?

*DEEPER EXPERIENCE*

> *"Man cannot control future events. He has neither the wisdom to see the future nor the power to control the future. For him to boast is sin; it is making himself God." (W. Weirsbe, Be Mature: Growing Up in Christ, p. 140).*

## EXPERIENCE 3: ENTRUSTING YOUR FINANCES TO GOD

James 5:1–6

1. Read James 5:1. What warning does James give? Who is he addressing?

2. Read James 5:2–3. What have the rich done with their wealth?

3. Read Matthew 6:19–21. How did Jesus warn the wealthy in these verses?

   a. Explain what Matthew meant when he said in verse 21, "Where your treasure is, there your heart will be also."

   b. Is wealth in and of itself bad? Explain.

4. Read James 5:4. A fraudulent behavior has occurred in this verse. What is it? Who has heard the outcries from the people who have been wronged?

"God is... the Lord of Sabaoth, that is, the Lord of hosts—a Hebrew word retained in the Greek, as James 5:4. All the hosts of heaven and earth are at His beck and disposal." (Ed note: and Jehovah of hosts is always open to our cry for help... What a mighty God we serve!) (Henry, M. Matthew Henry's Commentary on the Whole Bible, PreceptAustin.org)

5. Read the following verses and describe what God hears in heaven from the people on earth.

   Psalm 18:6

   Psalm 34:17

   1 Peter 3:12

6. Remember that James is writing to Jewish believers. They would have known what God commanded in the Law. Read Deuteronomy 24:14–15. How would they take comfort from these verses regarding their circumstances?

7. Read James 5:5. Describe the life of the wealthy in this verse.

8. Read James 5:6. What has happened to the just (poor) people? How did they respond to their treatment?

## DEEPER EXPERIENCE

9. Read 1 Timothy 6:10, 17–19. What do you learn about money and the challenges that wealth can bring in our walk with God?

    a. Use verses 17–19 to help explain how we can trust God with our finances.

## JESUS' EXAMPLE

When Jesus and Peter came to Capernaum, those who collected the temple tax asked Peter if Jesus was planning to pay his taxes. Jesus, not wanting to offend the tax collectors, told Peter to go down to the sea, cast out a fishing line, and a coin would be in the mouth of the first fish he caught. He was to then take that coin and pay the tax for both Peter and Him (Matthew 17:24–27). Jesus did not worry about money because he knew God would supply all of His needs. We too can trust God with our finances because God will supply all we need in accordance with His riches in glory through Christ Jesus (Philippians 4:19).

## EXPERIENCE 4: ENTRUSTING YOUR CIRCUMSTANCES TO GOD

James 5:7–12

1. James ends his letter to the Jewish believers similarly to how he began it in James 1:2–4. Compare and contrast how James encourages the Jewish believers once again.

a. Explain the parable James used to illustrate his point.

2. In 2 Corinthians 4:16–18 Paul echoes the same encouragements that James shared. What did Paul say about our circumstances and eternity?

3. Read James 5:9. As the Jewish believers are waiting on the Lord, what has been happening among them? What causes people to respond this way while they are waiting?

a. How is the Lord's return described in verse 9? Why should this be comforting for them as they endure under hard circumstances inflicted by others?

4. Read James 5:10–11. Why would James point to Old Testament prophets to help these believers endure difficulties?

5. James references Job in verse 11. Read Job 1:1–3, 13–22 and Job 2:7–8. Describe Job's suffering.

   a. Read Job 42:5–6, 10–12. How was the Lord compassionate and merciful to Job as described in James 5:11?

   b. Why would James use Job's story as one of encouragement?

6. Read James 5:12. James returns to the power of the tongue in regard to our response during trying circumstances. How does he instruct believers to use their mouths in trying times? Why would James give this instruction?

7. Summarize what you learned about a faith that trusts God.

*"It would be splendid if only we could say that this would never happen among Christians, that we never would use and never have used duplicity and misleading affirmations, promises and undertakings to get our own way, or to get ourselves out of a tight corner. It would be splendid if only we could say that we have never suffered from the white lies and intentionally misleading words and pledges of believers. It would be even more splendid if we had never been guilty ourselves."* (J.A. Motyer, The Message of James, pg. 184)

## ACTING ON GOD'S WORD

Trusting God is foundational to the Christian life. James was writing to believers who were facing various difficulties and unfair circumstances. He reminded them to keep eternity in perspective because life is but a vapor and is gone before we know it. Just like James encouraged believers at that time, trusting God is easier when we recognize our life and trials are allowed and controlled by Him.

Each day we have attitudes and actions that flow from us in response to our ever-changing circumstances. We may or may not like what unfolds, but our responses typically reflect our heart condition. If we want to develop more trust in God, we need to turn our eyes back upon the Lord and give everything back to Him. This is not easy; there are entire books written on the topic of trusting God. However, change always begins the same way; we must identify the problem. Let's spend some time asking God to show us where we are not trusting Him fully, and then set a plan into motion for how we can learn to trust Him more.

**HEAD** | **What do I know?**

1. List some of the topics that were addressed in James 4:11–5:12 that require trusting God.

2. Now, using your list from the previous page, circle a topic you want to see grow into a more God-honoring practice which reflects your trust in Him.

---

**HEART** | How is God moving in my heart?

1. Next, pray for a few moments about the topic you circled in the previous question. What is God asking you to change about your attitudes/actions?

2. Is there fear, control, or anxiety inhibiting your ability to trust God in the circumstance?

3. Have your attitudes/actions harmed your relationship with God? Explain.

4. Why might God desire this behavior to improve? What may result if nothing changes?

**HABIT**  How is God asking me to live out my faith?

1.  Write a few brief steps you would like to take the next time you find yourself tempted to fall into your old habit which God has identified needs to change.

2.  How will listening to the Holy Spirit be a necessary part of any lasting change?

3.  How will you use the Word of God to support your change?

4.  If you have a calendar, look ahead one week from now and set a reminder to check in with yourself to see how things are going. Typically, any lasting change needs practice for at least a few weeks in order for it to stick. If necessary, continue to move the reminder forward on your calendar and keep track of how God is making a change in the area you have identified. Be sure to praise and thank Him as you see the progress occurring!

## DELIGHTING IN GOD'S WORD

As you end this week's lesson, write down a verse that God has impressed upon your heart throughout the week and pray it back to the Lord.

Teaching Title _____

_____

_____

_____

_____

_____

_____

_____

_____

_____

_____

_____

_____

_____

_____

_____

_____

_____

_____

_____

_____

_____

_____

_____

Teaching Videos and handouts are available for free at www.delightinginthelord.com.

Teaching Title _____

_____

_____

_____

_____

_____

_____

_____

_____

_____

_____

_____

_____

_____

_____

_____

_____

_____

_____

_____

_____

_____

Teaching Videos and handouts are available for free at www.delightinginthelord.com.

# WEEK 9
# A Faith that Prays Fervently

His heart was pounding in his chest as Dr. David Levy, a neurosurgeon, entered the preoperative area. Although rarely nervous before surgery, this day he was terrified. He had made up his mind to pray with his patient, Mrs. Jones, before her surgery. The Lord had been directing him to ask his patients if he could pray for them as part of their medical care. This was not an easy decision as a neurosurgeon because matters of faith seemed firmly outside of his profession. It was as if those who were paid to operate on the body were somehow supposed to be above spirituality. Many of his colleagues felt that spiritual things were just silly superstitions used by the weak. David did not share this viewpoint. As a doctor, David considered himself a man of science, logic, and technology, but he also considered himself a follower of Christ and a man of God.

> WHEN WE HAVE PLACED OUR FAITH IN JESUS CHRIST, OUR PRAYERS HAVE AN IMPACT.

For years David had not been able to escape the overwhelming sense that God wanted to be invited into his professional life. Fear-filled questions ran through his mind. If he prayed for his patients, would it ruin his professional reputation? Would patients be offended if he asked to pray for them? If an operation went poorly, would it appear as though God hadn't heard his prayer? When the questions finally stopped swirling in his mind, he heard within his spirit, "If you are worried about being misunderstood, I can promise you that you will be. Jesus was. But you still need to do the right thing."

Shortly thereafter, David committed to pray for his very next patient, and Mrs. Jones was that patient! After reviewing the surgery plan with her, Dr. Levy mustered up all his courage and said, "Mrs. Jones, can I pray with you?" Mrs. Jones looked surprised, but her face softened, and she said, "Okay."

David's prayer was short and straightforward. He said,

*"God you've been with Mrs. Jones since she was a baby. You know all about her vessels, and I know that you can help me fix them. Please give me wisdom and skill. I ask for success in this surgery, in the name of Jesus, Amen."*

When David opened his eyes, Mrs. Jones was smiling peacefully, and tear stains rested on her cheeks. This prayer became the first of a career-long practice which incorporated prayer with each patient. Dr. Levy did not foresee what would evolve next.

For most of David's young adult life, he had held unforgiveness against his dad, despite the fact he knew it was medically proven that emotions affect the immune system and bitterness can inhibit healing. After David forgave his father, he experienced a joy and peace he believed would help his patients too. Dr. Levy added one simple question to the paperwork he collected when a new patient came to see him. It simply asked if they had withheld forgiveness from anyone. The response was astounding. Over the years Dr. Levy has helped many to forgive those who have hurt them and led some people into a time of confession and acceptance of Jesus as their Savior.

James writes, "The effectual fervent prayer of a righteous man avails much" (James 5:16). When we have placed our faith in Jesus Christ, our prayers have an impact. God invites us to pray about every trial, but we need to remember He has a purpose for what He has allowed. When he allows sickness and difficulty, we should pray fervently in faith and believe but also understand the results rest with Him. The text from this week's lesson is not an ironclad promise. It does not guarantee that just because you believe and pray for a healing, it will be delivered. Sometimes God says, "Yes," sometimes He may say, "No," and other times He will say, "Wait." May God encourage you this week to pray fervently and to have faith to trust Him with the outcome.

## RECEIVING GOD'S WORD

**Open in Prayer**
Read James 5:13–20

## EXPERIENCING GOD'S WORD

### EXPERIENCE 1: PRAYER OF FAITH

James 5:13–16a

1. Read James 5:13–14a. James identifies people in different situations. List them below and write James' command next to each group regarding their circumstance.

2. How do the commands in James 5:13–14 acknowledge God as the only resource for times of hardship and plenty?

   a. What phrase is repeated in these verses? What does this suggest about our response to God in these commands?

### DEEPER EXPERIENCE

*"Perhaps the two greatest weaknesses in the average church today are the areas of prayer and praise. The reason for these weaknesses may be traced to insensitivity. There is much need for prayer and much cause to praise. Suffering should elicit prayer. Sufficiency should elicit praise."* (Bible Knowledge Commentary: New Testament, p. 834)

3. In James 5:14 the elders of the church are given a command of how to help someone who is sick. What is this command?

4. Let's look at how the command in verse 14 aligns with God's heart. Read Mark 6:12–13. What did the disciples do when they were sent out by the Lord? How does this show us God's heart toward those who are physically sick?

## DEEPER EXPERIENCE

*"Anointing with oil has been interpreted as either seeking the best medical attention possible for the afflicted (oil massages were considered medicinal), or as an emblem of the Holy Spirit's presence and power." (David Guzik, blueletterbible.org)*

*"It is notable that the main verb in this section is the command to pray and anointing is a participle, so clearly anointing is not the main thrust but praying." (D. Edmond Hiebert, James Commentary quoted on PreceptAustin.org)*

5. How should the elders pray according to James 5:14b–15a?

   a. Verses 14b and 15a suggests the elders pray a certain way. How could the prayer look different? Why would this be a problem?

   b. How could God honor this type of prayer?

6. Let's look at what 1 John 5:14 says about our prayers to God. Read 1 John 5:14. What confidence does this verse give? What determines whether God chooses to heal someone or not?

7. Look up the following verses that illustrate God's will and power to heal in different situations. Let's see if He heals based on certain criteria. Match the verses with the statements below:

   Matthew 13:58          Healing not based on wealth

   John 5:1–9             Healing not based on faith

   John 5:13              No one healed

   Acts 3:2–6             One person healed among many

8. Death and sickness were not God's plan. Romans 5 tells us that death came through the sin of Adam in the Garden of Eden. And yet, it is God who gives all facets of life; physical, spiritual, and eternal. Life comes through God's Son, Jesus Christ. God had a plan from the beginning that aligned with His heart for all people. That plan culminates in a believer's eternal life with God. How do people sometimes lose sight of eternity when it comes to God's heart and healing?

9. Read James 5:15b and 1 John 1:9. Who forgives sin?

10. Considering James 5:14–15b and 1 John 1:9, what is James saying about sin and healing?

11. Are the prayer of faith, the oil, and forgiveness all requirements to healing? Explain.

12. Read James 5:16a. What does James recommend regarding those who are sick? Why would doing these two things be helpful toward healing?

## EXPERIENCE 2: THE FERVENT PRAYER

James 5:16b–18

1. Read James 5:16b. What does James say about prayer?

   a. James used the word *fervent* in 16b when describing prayer. The word *fervent* is *energeō* (Strong's G1754) which means to work and put forth power. Read Zechariah 4:6. Based on the definition above and this verse, where does the work and power come from to impact prayer?

2. Read James 5:17–18 and answer the following questions on Elijah's example:

   a. How is Elijah described? (v. 17)

b. What were the circumstances surrounding Elijah's prayer? (v. 17)

c. How is his prayer described? (v. 17–18)

d. How did God answer Elijah's prayer? (v.18)

3. Read 1 Kings 17:1–7 and 1 Kings 18:1. What do you learn from these verses that help you understand Elijah's prayer life? How do these prayers demonstrate he was praying God's will?

## DEEPER EXPERIENCE

*"We are apt to think of prophets and other servants of God mentioned in Holy Writ as men who were of a different fiber than we are, but they were all of the same family of frail humanity, men of like passions with us, but men who dared to believe God and give Him full control of their lives." (H.A. Ironside, James and 1 and 2 Peter, p.47)*

4. What do you learn from the following verses about prayer?

2 Chronicles 7:14

Matthew 6:6–13

Philippians 4:6–7

1 Thessalonians 5:17

## JESUS' EXAMPLE

*Jesus spent His days in Galilee walking the streets, teaching, and doing miraculous works. Many followed Him each day, desiring even a morsel of what He offered. Despite His deep compassion and love for everyone, there were those in the religious elite who became enraged at His works. His opposition grew quickly. Jesus' days were long and full. Even Jesus needed to pray to His Father. "Now it came to pass in those days that He went out to the mountain to pray; and continued all night in prayer to God" (Luke 6:12). Jesus prayed fervently, knowing prayer aligned His will with God's.*

## EXPERIENCE 3: RESTORATION

James 5:19–20

1. Read James 5:19–20. Throughout this book James has exhorted believers in their walk of faith. If you are truly a believer in Jesus Christ, your life will reflect that choice. James ends by challenging believers regarding those around them who say they are a believer but their choices don't testify to that belief. What is a believer's responsibility according to these verses? What is at stake if they do not seek out someone who has wandered from the truth?

2. Read Ephesians 4:15. If you must restore another person, how should the truth be shared? What can result?

3. James tells us we need to care for those around us. Read the following verses and note what you learn about how to care for those who say they are in the body of Christ.

1 Corinthians 12:25–26

Galatians 6:1–2

Galatians 6:9–10

1 Timothy 2:1–2

4. Read Philippians 2:3–4. How does pride and humility affect our ability to care for the body of Christ?

5. Read Matthew 18:12–14. How does this parable echo the encouragement James gives in James 5:19–20?

## JESUS' EXAMPLE

Breakfast was over and Jesus looked at Peter. There was a lingering sense of unresolved sin. The night before Jesus' death Peter denied knowing Jesus three times, just as Jesus had predicted. Peter was so remorseful over the betrayal. Jesus asked Peter three times if he loved Him, and then said, "Follow Me." (John 21:19). Restoration had been extended to Peter, and as a result, Peter would go on to become one of the most influential men in the early church. Without this restoration, Peter may have chosen to wander from the truth. May we follow Jesus' example and pursue restoration with others even when it means extending grace when we feel it may not be deserved.

6. Read 1 Peter 4:7–11. How do these verses summarize all James has been describing in James 5:13–20?

## DEEPER EXPERIENCE

*"James concludes with this because this is exactly what he has endeavored to do through this challenging letter—to confront those who have wandered from a living faith, endeavoring to save their souls from death, by demanding that they not only hear the word, but do it, because a living faith will have its proof." (David Guzik, blueletterbible.org)*

## ACTING ON GOD'S WORD

If I (Stacy) were to guess, I would say that we have all experienced disease in some capacity. For some, it may be personal to our own body; for others, it may be the sickness of a loved one. For many of us, it's both. As James started this letter with the topic of suffering, he now comes full circle by also ending with it. He has brought us on a spiritual progression of faith while overlapping topics throughout his letter. He has shown us what active, saving faith should look like in many areas of life as we walk out our faith.

He ends with a believer's prayer life. Prayer is an outworking of our faith. As James said, it should be "fervent." He had us look at the use of prayer when we are dealing with disease. He also challenged us with prayer regarding the body of Christ. Prayer must be our go-to weapon in the valley of suffering just as worship is our go-to cry on the mountaintop of bliss. We need to be careful to not just keep our eyes on our own circumstances, but to also look around us for those who may be suffering too. We are in this life of faith together, in community, and we need each other. We can't lose sight of that.

James has also challenged us to not lose sight of eternity in the days God gives each of us. In the previous verses (5:7–12), James reminded us of this. It is only natural for this truth to overflow into disease and healing. I think it might be one of the reasons we may struggle with this area so much. We often have too tight of a grip on this world. We want healing so we can stay in the world a little longer. I know I've been guilty of this thought process. And yet, what is waiting for us in eternity is no doubt so much better than anything this life offers.

As we wrap up our study on the book of James, let's look at our prayer life in the midst of suffering and apply James' teaching to our lives.

**HEAD** | What do I know?

1. Is there anything you learned about God and His desire for you regarding prayer?

2. What did you learn about God's interaction with those who are sick?

3. What did you learn about how your prayers impact the body of Christ, especially when they are suffering?

**HEART** | How is God moving in my heart?

1. How did God encourage you from James 5:13–20?

2. Is God exposing any sin in your life as you studied these verses?

3. How do your heart attitudes and actions respond to disease?

4. Do you put any unspoken expectations on the Lord and how He chooses to intervene in sicknesses you or a loved one experiences? Explain.

HABIT | **How is God asking me to live out my faith?**

1. Make an honest assessment of your prayer life. Would God say you pray fervently? How can you make changes to your prayer life to support James' teaching in 5:13–18?

2. Does your thinking on prayer and healing align with what God's Word teaches? What changes may need to be made so that your life can reflect the truth of God in this area?

3. How is your faith demonstrated in your care of those in the body of Christ, especially with those suffering or who have wandered from the Lord? What can you do today that would encourage a brother or sister who is sick or wayward?

4. How has the book of James impacted your faith and walk with the Lord?

## DELIGHTING IN GOD'S WORD

As you end this week's lesson, write down a verse that God has impressed upon your heart throughout the week and pray it back to the Lord.

Teaching Title _____

_____

_____

_____

_____

_____

_____

_____

_____

_____

_____

_____

_____

_____

_____

_____

_____

_____

_____

_____

_____

_____

_____

Teaching Videos and handouts are available for free at www.delightinginthelord.com.

Teaching Title _____

_____

_____

_____

_____

_____

_____

_____

_____

_____

_____

_____

_____

_____

_____

_____

_____

_____

_____

_____

_____

Teaching Videos and handouts are available for free at www.delightinginthelord.com.

Ironside, H.A. *James and 1 and 2 Peter: An Ironside Expository Commentary*. Kregel Publications, 2008.

Levy, David I. and Joel Kilpatrick. *Gray Matter*. Tyndale House Publishers, 2011.

Mcgee, J. Vernon. *The Epistles: James*. Thomas Nelson, 1955.

Miller, B. *George Müller: The Man of Faith*. Zondervan Publishing House, 1941.

Motyer, J. A. *The Message of James* (The Bible Speaks Today Series). Inter-Varsity Press, 1985.

Phillips, John. *Exploring the Epistle of James: An Expository Commentary*. Kregel Publications, 2004.

Ripken, Nik, and Gregg Lewis. *The Insanity of God: a True Story of Faith Resurrected*. B & H Publishing Group, 2013.

Walvoord, John F., and Roy B. Zuck. *The Bible Knowledge Commentary: New Testament*. David C. Cook, 1983.

Wiersbe, Warren W. *Be Mature (James): Growing Up in Christ*. David C. Cook, 2008.

Wilkerson, David, et al. *The Cross and the Switchblade*. Jove Books, 1962.

www.blueletterbible.org

www.dictionary.cambridge.org

www.drandrewjackson.com/the-new-testament-letter-of colossians-and-the-site-of-colossae-in-modern-turkey/

www.harvestministry.org/muller

www.npr.org/templates/story/story.php?storyid=11762186

www.preceptaustin.org

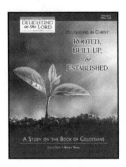

Delighting In Christ: Rooted, Built Up, and Established
A Study on the Book of Colossians (Amazon)
*9 Week Study*

This study addresses Christ's preeminence over all areas of the believer's life. Paul warns the church at Colossae to beware of false teachings by reinforcing the truth of Jesus Christ. The study encourages those who follow Jesus to be rooted, built up, and established in Him.

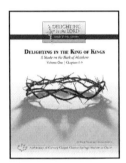

Delighting in the King of Kings: Matthew Volume 1: Chapters 1–9 (Amazon) *9 Weeks*
Delighting in the King of Kings: Matthew Volume 2: Chapters 10–20 (Amazon) *11 Weeks*
Delighting in the King of Kings: Matthew Volume 3: Chapters 21–28 (Amazon) *8 Weeks*
*28 Week Study Total*

Study the life of the King of Kings, Jesus Christ, from His birth to His ascension from the perspective of the gospel writer Matthew. This series is written as a three-volume set but can be studied individually.

Delighting in God's Wisdom: Proverbs (Amazon)
*13 Week Study*

Gain wisdom from the book of Proverbs while learning from examples of women in the Bible. King Solomon is the primary writer of this book and sets forth insights on how to solve many of life's challenges.

**Delighting in a Life of Triumph: A Study on the Life of Joseph from Genesis 37–50 (Amazon)**
*9 Week Study*

Examine what triumphant living can look like, even when faced with challenging family relationships, being wrongly accused, and forgotten by those who should have loved you. The life of Joseph is a powerful testimony about how to live victoriously amidst life's difficult circumstances.

**Delighting in a Life Lived for God: A Study on the Book of 1 Peter (Amazon)**
*10 Week Study*

Study the encouragement given by the disciple Peter on how to live a perfected, established, strengthened, and settled life in the Lord while in the midst of difficulty, trials, and persecution.

**Delighting in Being a Woman of God: Esther**
**(Revised edition available on Amazon Fall 2021)**
*8 Week Study*

See how God impacted the entire Jewish nation through the life of one God-ordained woman named Esther. This study reminds us that God can use anyone who is obedient to His call to impact their generation.

Additional verse-by-verse studies can be found at www.delightinginthelord.com. These studies were used in the women's ministry at Calvary Chapel Chester Springs. Any study can be downloaded for free from the Delighting in the Lord ministry website. Each study has video teachings that accompany the weekly lessons.

*The studies are:*

Delighting in the Holy Spirit: Acts
*26 Week Study*

Delighting in God's Heart: The Life of David through 1 & 2 Samuel and the Psalms
*24 Week Study*

Delighting in the Redeemer: A Love Story from the book of Ruth
*4 Week Study*

Delighting in God's Will and His Provision: Jonah & Nahum
*7 Week Study*

Delighting in God, His Righteousness, and Perfect Plan: Romans
*17 Week Study*

**For additional information about the ministry, please go to:**

www.delightinginthelord.com
www.cc-chestersprings.com/resources/ditl-series

***For weekly encouragement, follow Delighting in the Lord on Facebook***

Made in United States
Orlando, FL
28 October 2024